To my SWEETHEART ELSIE

LOVE DEAN

SLOW COOKER
RECIPES

Publications International, Ltd.

Table of Contents

Slow Cooking Tips

Sizes of CROCK-POT®
Slow Cookers

Smaller **CROCK-POT®** slow cookers—such as 1- to 3½-quart models—are the perfect size for cooking for singles, a couple or empty nesters (and also for serving dips).

While medium-size **CROCK-POT®** slow cookers (those holding somewhere between 3 quarts and 5 quarts) will easily cook enough food at a time to feed a small family. They are also convenient for holiday side dishes or appetizers.

Large **CROCK-POT®** slow cookers are great for large family dinners, holiday entertaining and potluck suppers. A 6- to 7-quart model is ideal if you like to make meals in advance, or have dinner tonight and store leftovers for another day.

Types of CROCK-POT®
Slow Cookers

Current **CROCK-POT®** slow cookers come equipped with many different features and benefits, from auto cook programs to oven-safe stoneware to timed programming. Please visit **WWW.CROCK-POT.COM** to find the **CROCK-POT®** slow cooker that best suits your needs.

How you plan to use a **CROCK-POT®** slow cooker may affect the model you choose to purchase. For everyday cooking, choose a size large enough to serve your family. If you plan to use the **CROCK-POT®** slow cooker primarily for entertaining, choose one of the larger sizes. Basic **CROCK-POT®** slow cookers can hold as little as 16 ounces or as much as 7 quarts. The smallest sizes are great for keeping dips warm on a buffet, while the larger sizes can more readily fit large quantities of food and larger roasts.

Cooking, Stirring and Food Safety

CROCK-POT® slow cookers are safe to leave unattended. The outer heating base may get hot as it cooks, but it should not pose a fire hazard. The heating element in the heating base functions at a low wattage and is safe for your countertops.

Your **CROCK-POT**® slow cooker should be filled about one-half to three-fourths full for most recipes unless otherwise instructed. Lean meats such as chicken or pork tenderloin will cook faster than meats with more connective tissue and fat such as beef chuck or pork shoulder. Bone-in meats will take longer than boneless cuts. Typical **CROCK-POT**® slow cooker dishes take approximately 7 to 8 hours to reach the simmer point on LOW and about 3 to 4 hours on HIGH. Once the vegetables and meat start to simmer and braise, their flavors will fully blend and meat will become fall-off-the-bone tender.

According to the U.S. Department of Agriculture, all bacteria are killed at a temperature of 165°F. It's important to follow the recommended cooking times and not to open the lid often, especially early in the cooking process when heat is building up inside the unit. If you need to open the lid to check on your food or are adding additional ingredients, remember to allow additional cooking time if necessary to ensure food is cooked through and tender.

Large **CROCK-POT**® slow cookers, the 6- to 7-quart sizes, may benefit from a quick stir halfway through cook time to help distribute heat and promote even cooking. It's usually unnecessary to stir at all, as even ½ cup liquid will help to distribute heat and the stoneware is the perfect medium for holding food at an even temperature throughout the cooking process.

Oven-Safe Stoneware

All **CROCK-POT**® slow cooker removable stoneware inserts may (without their lids) be used safely in ovens at up to 400°F. In addition, all **CROCK-POT**® slow cookers are microwavable without their lids. If you own another slow cooker brand, please refer to your owner's manual for specific stoneware cooking medium tolerances.

Frozen Food

Frozen food can be successfully cooked in a **CROCK-POT**® slow cooker. However, it will require longer cooking time than the same recipe made with fresh food. It's almost always preferable to thaw frozen food prior to placing it in the **CROCK-POT**® slow cooker. Using an instant-read thermometer is recommended to ensure meat is fully cooked through.

Pasta and Rice

If you are converting a recipe for a **CROCK-POT**® slow cooker that calls for uncooked pasta, first cook the pasta on the stovetop just until slightly tender. Then add the pasta to the **CROCK-POT**® slow cooker. If you are converting a recipe for the **CROCK-POT**® slow cooker that calls for cooked rice, stir in raw rice with the other recipe ingredients plus ¼ cup extra liquid per ¼ cup of raw rice.

Beans

Beans must be softened completely before combining with sugar and/or acidic foods in the **CROCK-POT**® slow cooker. Sugar and acid have a hardening effect on beans and will prevent softening. Fully cooked canned beans may be used as a substitute for dried beans.

Vegetables

Root vegetables often cook more slowly than meat. Cut vegetables accordingly to cook at the same rate as meat—large or small or lean versus marbled—and place near the sides or bottom of the stoneware to facilitate cooking.

Herbs

Fresh herbs add flavor and color when added at the end of the cooking cycle; if added at the beginning, many fresh herbs' flavor will dissipate over long cook times. Ground and/or dried herbs and spices work well in slow cooking and may be added at the beginning of cook time. For dishes with shorter cook times, hearty fresh herbs such as rosemary and thyme hold up well. The flavor power of all herbs and spices can vary greatly depending on their particular strength and shelf life. Use chili powders and garlic powder sparingly, as these can sometimes intensify over the long cook times. Always taste the finished dish and correct seasonings including salt and pepper.

Liquids

It's not necessary to use more than ½ to 1 cup liquid in most instances since juices in meats and vegetables are retained more in slow cooking than in conventional cooking. Excess liquid can be cooked down and concentrated after slow cooking on the stovetop or by removing meat and vegetables from stoneware, stirring in one of the following thickeners and setting the **CROCK-POT**® slow cooker to HIGH. Cover; cook on HIGH for approximately 15 minutes or until juices are thickened.

FLOUR: All-purpose flour is often used to thicken soups or stews. Stir cold water into the flour in a small bowl until smooth. With the **CROCK-POT**® slow cooker on HIGH, whisk the flour mixture into the liquid in the **CROCK-POT**® slow cooker. Cover; cook on HIGH 15 minutes or until the mixture is thickened.

CORNSTARCH: Cornstarch gives sauces a clear, shiny appearance; it's used most often for sweet dessert sauces and stir-fry sauces. Stir cold water into the cornstarch in a small bowl until the cornstarch dissolves. Quickly stir this mixture into the liquid in the **CROCK-POT**® slow cooker; the sauce will thicken as soon as the liquid simmers. Cornstarch breaks down with too much heat, so never add it at the beginning of the slow cooking process and turn off the heat as soon as the sauce thickens.

ARROWROOT: Arrowroot (or arrowroot flour) comes from the root of a tropical plant that is dried and ground to a powder; it produces a thick, clear sauce. Those who are allergic to wheat often use it in place of flour. Place arrowroot in a small bowl or cup and stir in cold water until the mixture is smooth. Quickly stir this mixture into the liquid in the **CROCK-POT**® slow cooker. Arrowroot thickens below the boiling point, so it even works well in a **CROCK-POT**® slow cooker on LOW. Too much stirring can break down an arrowroot mixture.

TAPIOCA: Tapioca is a starchy substance extracted from the root of the cassava plant. Its greatest advantage is that it withstands long cooking, making it an ideal choice for slow cooking. Add it at the beginning of cooking and you'll get a clear, thickened sauce in the finished dish. Dishes using tapioca as a thickener are best cooked on the LOW setting; tapioca may become stringy when boiled for a long time.

Milk

Milk, cream and sour cream break down during extended cooking. When possible, add them during the last 15 to 30 minutes of slow cooking, until just heated through. Condensed soups may be substituted for milk and may cook for extended times.

Fish

Fish is delicate and should be stirred into the **CROCK-POT**® slow cooker gently during the last 15 to 30 minutes of cooking time. Cover; cook just until cooked through and serve immediately.

Baked Goods

If you wish to prepare bread, cakes or pudding cakes in a **CROCK-POT**® slow cooker, you may want to purchase a covered, vented metal cake pan accessory for your **CROCK-POT**® slow cooker. You can also use any straight-sided soufflé dish or deep cake pan that will fit into the stoneware of your unit. Baked goods can be prepared directly in the stoneware; however, they can be a little difficult to remove from the insert, so follow the recipe directions carefully.

Amazing Appetizers

Easiest Three-Cheese Fondue

2 cups (8 ounces) shredded Cheddar cheese

¾ cup milk

½ cup crumbled blue cheese

1 package (3 ounces) cream cheese, cut into cubes

¼ cup finely chopped onion

1 tablespoon all-purpose flour

1 tablespoon butter

2 cloves garlic, minced

4 to 6 drops hot pepper sauce

⅛ teaspoon ground red pepper

Breadsticks and assorted cut-up fresh vegetables

1. Combine Cheddar cheese, milk, blue cheese, cream cheese, onion, flour, butter, garlic, hot pepper sauce and ground red pepper in **CROCK-POT**® slow cooker. Cover; cook on LOW 2 to 2½ hours, stirring halfway through cooking time.

2. Turn **CROCK-POT**® slow cooker to HIGH. Cover; cook on HIGH 1 to 1½ hours or until heated through. Serve with breadsticks and vegetables.

MAKES 8 SERVINGS

Warm Blue Crab Bruschetta

4 cups peeled seeded and diced plum tomatoes

1 cup diced white onion

⅓ cup olive oil

2 tablespoons sugar

2 tablespoons balsamic vinegar

2 teaspoons minced garlic

½ teaspoon dried oregano

1 pound lump blue crabmeat, picked over for shells

1½ teaspoons kosher salt

½ teaspoon cracked black pepper

⅓ cup minced fresh basil

2 baguettes, sliced and toasted

1. Combine tomatoes, onion, oil, sugar, vinegar, garlic and oregano in **CROCK-POT®** slow cooker. Cover; cook on LOW 2 hours.

2. Stir crabmeat, salt and pepper into **CROCK-POT®** slow cooker, taking care not to break up crabmeat. Cover; cook on LOW 1 hour. Fold in basil. Serve on baguette slices.

MAKES 16 SERVINGS

SERVING SUGGESTIONS: Crab topping can also be served on Melba toast or whole grain crackers.

Brats in Beer

1½ pounds bratwurst (5 to 6 links)
1 can (12 ounces) amber ale or beer
1 onion, thinly sliced
2 tablespoons packed brown sugar

2 tablespoons dry red wine or cider vinegar
Spicy brown mustard
Cocktail rye bread

1. Combine bratwurst, ale, onion, brown sugar and vinegar in **CROCK-POT**® slow cooker. Cover; cook on LOW 4 to 5 hours.

2. Remove bratwurst from cooking liquid. Cut into ½-inch-thick slices. Spread mustard on bread. Top with bratwurst slices and onion.

MAKES 30 TO 36 SERVINGS

TIP: Choose a light-colored beer when cooking brats. Hearty ales can leave the meat tasting slightly bitter.

Asian Barbecue Skewers

2 pounds boneless, skinless chicken thighs

½ cup soy sauce

⅓ cup packed brown sugar

2 tablespoons sesame oil

3 cloves garlic, minced

1 tablespoon toasted sesame seeds (optional)*

To toast sesame seeds, spread in small skillet. Shake skillet over medium-low heat 2 minutes or until seeds begin to pop and turn golden brown.

1. Cut each chicken thigh into four pieces, about 1½ inches thick. Thread chicken onto 7-inch-long wooden skewers, folding thinner pieces, if necessary. Place skewers into **CROCK-POT**® slow cooker, layering as flat as possible.

2. Combine soy sauce, brown sugar, oil and garlic in small bowl; stir to blend. Reserve ⅓ cup sauce. Pour remaining sauce over skewers. Cover; cook on LOW 2 hours. Turn skewers over. Cover; cook on LOW 1 hour.

3. Remove skewers to large serving platter. Discard cooking liquid. Pour reserved sauce over skewers. Sprinkle with sesame seeds, if desired.

MAKES 4 TO 6 SERVINGS

Juicy Reuben Sliders

1 corned beef brisket (about 1½ pounds), trimmed

2 cups sauerkraut, drained

½ cup beef broth

1 small onion, sliced

1 clove garlic, minced

4 to 6 whole white peppercorns

¼ teaspoon caraway seeds

48 slices pumpernickel or cocktail rye bread

12 slices deli Swiss cheese

Dijon mustard (optional)

1. Place corned beef in **CROCK-POT**® slow cooker. Add sauerkraut, broth, onion, garlic, peppercorns and caraway seeds. Cover; cook on LOW 7 to 9 hours.

2. Remove corned beef to large cutting board. Cut across grain into 16 slices. Cut each slice into 3 pieces. Place 2 pieces corned beef on each of 24 slices of bread. Place 1 heaping tablespoon sauerkraut on each sandwich. Cut each slice of Swiss cheese into quarters; place 2 quarters on each sandwich. Spread remaining 24 slices of bread with mustard, if desired, and place on top of sandwiches.

MAKES 24 SLIDERS

Spicy Sweet and Sour Cocktail Franks

2 packages (8 ounces *each*) cocktail franks

½ cup ketchup or chili sauce

½ cup apricot preserves

1 teaspoon hot pepper sauce

Combine cocktail franks, ketchup, preserves and hot pepper sauce in 1½-quart **CROCK-POT**® slow cooker; mix well. Cover; cook on LOW 2 to 3 hours.

MAKES 10 TO 12 SERVINGS

Juicy Reuben Sliders

Raspberry-Balsamic Glazed Meatballs

1 bag (2 pounds) frozen fully cooked meatballs

1 cup raspberry preserves

3 tablespoons sugar

3 tablespoons balsamic vinegar

1 tablespoon plus 1½ teaspoons Worcestershire sauce

¼ teaspoon red pepper flakes

1 tablespoon grated fresh ginger (optional)

Sliced green onions (optional)

1. Coat inside of **CROCK-POT®** slow cooker with nonstick cooking spray. Add frozen meatballs.

2. Combine preserves, sugar, vinegar, Worcestershire sauce and red pepper flakes in small microwavable bowl. Microwave on HIGH 45 seconds; stir. Microwave 15 seconds or until melted. Reserve ½ cup glaze in refrigerator. Pour remaining glaze mixture over meatballs; stir until well coated. Cover; cook on LOW 5 hours or on HIGH 2½ hours.

3. Stir in reserved glaze and ginger, if desired. Cook, uncovered, on HIGH 15 to 20 minutes or until thickened slightly, stirring occasionally. Sprinkle each serving with green onions, if desired.

MAKES ABOUT 16 SERVINGS

Tomato Topping for Bruschetta

6 medium tomatoes, peeled, seeded and diced

2 stalks celery, chopped

2 shallots, chopped

4 pepperoncini peppers, chopped*

2 tablespoons olive oil

2 teaspoons tomato paste

1 teaspoon salt

½ teaspoon black pepper

8 slices country bread or other large round bread

2 cloves garlic, cut in half

Pepperoncini are pickled peppers sold in jars with brine. They are available in the condiment aisle of large supermarkets.

1. Drain tomatoes in fine mesh strainer. Combine tomatoes, celery, shallots, pepperoncini peppers, oil, tomato paste, salt and black pepper in **CROCK-POT**® slow cooker. Cover; cook on LOW 45 minutes to 1 hour.

2. Toast bread; immediately rub with garlic. Spread tomato topping on bread to serve.

MAKES 8 SERVINGS

Sausage and Swiss Chard Stuffed Mushrooms

4 tablespoons olive oil, divided

½ pound bulk pork sausage

½ onion, finely chopped

2 cups chopped Swiss chard

¼ teaspoon dried thyme

2 tablespoons garlic-and-herb-flavored dried bread crumbs

1½ cups chicken broth, divided

½ teaspoon salt, divided

½ teaspoon black pepper, divided

2 packages (6 ounces *each*) cremini mushrooms, stemmed*

2 tablespoons grated Parmesan cheese

2 tablespoons chopped fresh Italian parsley

Do not substitute with white button mushrooms.

1. Coat inside of **CROCK-POT**® slow cooker with nonstick cooking spray. Heat 1 tablespoon oil in medium skillet over medium heat. Add sausage; cook and stir 6 to 8 minutes or until browned. Remove sausage to medium bowl using slotted spoon.

2. Add onion to skillet; cook and stir 3 minutes or until translucent, scraping up any browned bits from bottom of skillet. Stir in Swiss chard and thyme; cook 1 to 2 minutes or until Swiss chard is wilted. Remove from heat.

3. Stir in sausage, bread crumbs, 1 tablespoon broth, ¼ teaspoon salt and ¼ teaspoon pepper. Brush remaining 3 tablespoons oil over mushrooms. Season with remaining ¼ teaspoon salt and ¼ teaspoon pepper. Fill mushrooms evenly with stuffing.

4. Pour remaining broth into **CROCK-POT**® slow cooker. Arrange stuffed mushrooms in bottom. Cover; cook on HIGH 3 hours. To serve, remove mushrooms using slotted spoon; discard cooking liquid. Combine cheese and parsley in small bowl; sprinkle evenly over mushrooms.

MAKES 6 TO 8 SERVINGS

Shrimp Fondue Dip

1 pound medium raw shrimp,
  peeled and deveined

½ cup water

½ teaspoon salt, divided

2 tablespoons butter, softened

4 teaspoons Dijon mustard

6 slices thick-sliced white bread,
  crusts removed*

1 cup milk

2 eggs, beaten

¼ teaspoon black pepper

2 cups (8 ounces) shredded Gruyère
  or Swiss cheese

French bread slices

*Often labeled as Texas toast.

1. Coat inside of **CROCK-POT®** slow cooker with nonstick cooking spray. Place shrimp, water and ¼ teaspoon salt in large saucepan. Cover; cook over medium heat 3 minutes or until shrimp are pink and opaque. Drain shrimp, reserving ½ cup broth.

2. Combine butter and mustard in small bowl; stir to blend. Spread mixture onto bread slices. Cut bread into 1-inch cubes. Beat milk, eggs, reserved ½ cup broth, remaining ¼ teaspoon salt and pepper in medium bowl until well blended.

3. Spread one third of bread cubes in bottom of **CROCK-POT®** slow cooker. Top with one third of shrimp and sprinkle with one third of cheese. Repeat layers twice. Pour egg mixture over top. Press down on bread mixture to absorb liquid. Line lid with two paper towels. Cover; cook on LOW 2 hours or until mixture is heated through and thickened. Serve on French bread.

MAKES 5 CUPS

TIP: For a party, use a **CROCK-POT®** slow cooker on the LOW or WARM setting to keep hot dips and fondues warm.

Apricot and Brie Dip

½ cup dried apricots, finely chopped

⅓ cup plus 1 tablespoon apricot preserves, divided

¼ cup apple juice

1 round wheel Brie cheese (2 pounds), rind removed and cut into cubes

Crackers or bread

Combine dried apricots, ⅓ cup apricot preserves and apple juice in **CROCK-POT**® slow cooker. Cover; cook on HIGH 40 minutes. Stir in cheese. Cover; cook on HIGH 30 to 40 minutes or until cheese is melted. Stir in remaining 1 tablespoon preserves. Turn **CROCK-POT**® slow cooker to LOW. Serve warm with crackers.

MAKES 3 CUPS

Lemon & Garlic Shrimp

1 pound large raw shrimp, peeled and deveined

½ cup (1 stick) unsalted butter, cubed

3 cloves garlic, crushed

2 tablespoons lemon juice

½ teaspoon paprika

Salt and black pepper

2 tablespoons finely chopped fresh Italian parsley

Crusty bread, sliced

1. Coat inside of **CROCK-POT**® slow cooker with nonstick cooking spray. Add shrimp, butter and garlic; stir to blend. Cover; cook on HIGH 1¼ hours.

2. Turn off heat. Stir in lemon juice, paprika, salt and pepper. Spoon shrimp and liquid into large serving bowl. Sprinkle with parsley. Serve with crusty bread for dipping.

MAKES 6 TO 8 SERVINGS

Apricot and Brie Dip

Asian Chicken Fondue

2 cups chicken broth

1 cup shiitake mushrooms, stems removed

1 leek, chopped

1 head baby bok choy, coarsely chopped

2 tablespoons oyster sauce

1 tablespoon mirin

1 tablespoon teriyaki sauce

2 pounds boneless, skinless chicken breasts, cut into 1-inch cubes

Salt and black pepper

1 tablespoon canola oil

1 cup seeded cubed butternut squash

2 tablespoons cold water

1 tablespoon cornstarch

1 can (8 ounces) baby corn, drained

1 can (8 ounces) water chestnuts, drained

1. Combine broth, mushrooms, leek, bok choy, oyster sauce, mirin and teriyaki sauce in **CROCK-POT**® slow cooker; stir to blend. Cover; cook on LOW while following remaining instructions.

2. Season chicken with salt and pepper. Heat oil in large skillet over medium-high heat. Add chicken; cook and stir 8 minutes or until lightly browned. Stir into **CROCK-POT**® slow cooker. Stir in squash. Cover; cook on LOW 4 to 4½ hours.

3. Stir water into cornstarch in small bowl until smooth. Stir baby corn and water chestnuts into **CROCK-POT**® slow cooker. Whisk in cornstarch mixture.

4. Cover; cook on LOW 20 to 30 minutes. Serve with bamboo skewers, fondue forks or tongs.

MAKES 6 TO 8 SERVINGS

Bacon-Wrapped Fingerling Potatoes

1 pound fingerling potatoes
2 tablespoons olive oil
1 tablespoon minced fresh thyme
½ teaspoon black pepper
¼ teaspoon paprika
½ pound bacon slices, cut crosswise into halves
¼ cup chicken broth

1. Toss potatoes with oil, thyme, pepper and paprika in large bowl. Wrap half slice of bacon tightly around each potato.

2. Heat large skillet over medium heat; add potatoes. Reduce heat to medium-low; cook until lightly browned and bacon has tightened around potatoes. Place potatoes in **CROCK-POT**® slow cooker. Add broth. Cover; cook on HIGH 3 hours.

MAKES 4 TO 6 SERVINGS

Salsa-Style Wings

2 tablespoons oil
1½ pounds chicken wings (about 18 wings)
2 cups salsa
¼ cup packed brown sugar
Sprigs fresh cilantro (optional)

1. Heat oil in large skillet over medium-high heat. Add wings in batches; cook 3 to 4 minutes or until browned on all sides. Remove to **CROCK-POT**® slow cooker.

2. Combine salsa and brown sugar in medium bowl; stir to blend. Pour over wings. Cover; cook on LOW 5 to 6 hours or on HIGH 2 to 3 hours. Serve with salsa mixture. Garnish with cilantro.

MAKES 4 SERVINGS

Bacon-Wrapped Fingerling Potatoes

Chicken and Asiago Stuffed Mushrooms

20 large white mushrooms, stems removed and reserved

3 tablespoons extra virgin olive oil, divided

¼ cup finely chopped onion

2 cloves garlic, minced

¼ cup Madeira wine

½ pound uncooked chicken sausage, casings removed or ground chicken

1 cup grated Asiago cheese

¼ cup Italian-style seasoned dry bread crumbs

3 tablespoons chopped fresh Italian parsley

½ teaspoon salt

¼ teaspoon black pepper

1. Lightly brush mushroom caps with 1 tablespoon oil; set aside. Finely chop mushroom stems.

2. Heat remaining 2 tablespoons oil in large skillet over medium-high heat. Add onion; cook 1 minute or until just beginning to soften. Add mushroom stems; cook 5 to 6 minutes or until beginning to brown. Stir in garlic; cook 1 minute.

3. Pour in wine; cook 1 minute. Add sausage; cook 3 to 4 minutes or until no longer pink, stirring to break into small pieces. Remove from heat; cool 5 minutes. Stir in cheese, bread crumbs, parsley, salt and pepper.

4. Divide mushroom-sausage mixture among mushroom caps, pressing slightly to compress. Place stuffed mushroom caps in single layer in **CROCK-POT**® slow cooker. Cover; cook on LOW 4 hours or on HIGH 2 hours.

MAKES 4 TO 5 SERVINGS

TIP: Stuffed mushrooms are a great way to impress guests with your gourmet home-cooking skills. These appetizers appear time-intensive and fancy, but they are actually simple with the help of a **CROCK-POT**® slow cooker.

Chicken Liver Pâté

1½ pounds chicken livers, trimmed of fat and membrane

1 small onion, thinly sliced

3 sprigs fresh thyme

2 cloves garlic, crushed

¼ teaspoon salt, plus additional for seasoning

1 tablespoon water

3 tablespoons cold butter, cut into 4 pieces

2 tablespoons whipping cream

2 tablespoons dry sherry

½ shallot, minced

2 tablespoons chopped fresh Italian parsley

1 tablespoon sherry vinegar

⅛ teaspoon sugar

Black pepper

Melba toast and crackers

1. Rinse chicken livers and pat dry. Place in **CROCK-POT®** slow cooker. Add onion, thyme, garlic, ¼ teaspoon salt and water. Cover; cook on LOW 2 hours.

2. Remove and discard thyme sprigs. Pour cooking liquid into food processor or blender; pulse to coarsely chop livers. Add butter, one piece at a time, pulsing after each addition just to combine.

3. Add whipping cream and sherry; pulse to combine. Remove to small loaf pan, pressing plastic wrap to surface of pâté. Refrigerate overnight, tightly wrapped in additional plastic wrap. Unmold pâté and slice to serve.

4. Combine shallot, parsley, vinegar and sugar in small bowl. Season with additional salt and pepper; stir to blend. Set aside 5 minutes. Spoon shallot mixture over pâté. Serve with Melba toast.

MAKES 8 TO 10 SERVINGS

Mini Tacos de Carnitas

1½ pounds boneless pork loin, cut into 1-inch cubes

1 onion, finely chopped

½ cup chicken broth

1 tablespoon chili powder

2 teaspoons ground cumin

1 teaspoon dried oregano

½ teaspoon minced canned chipotle peppers in adobo sauce

½ cup pico de gallo

2 tablespoons chopped fresh cilantro

½ teaspoon salt

12 (6-inch) corn or flour tortillas

¾ cup (3 ounces) shredded sharp Cheddar cheese

3 tablespoons sour cream

1. Combine pork, onion, broth, chili powder, cumin, oregano and chipotle peppers in **CROCK-POT®** slow cooker; stir to blend. Cover; cook on LOW 6 hours or on HIGH 3 hours. Pour off excess cooking liquid.

2. Remove pork to large cutting board; shred with two forks. Return to **CROCK-POT®** slow cooker. Stir in pico de gallo, cilantro and salt. Cover; keep warm on LOW or WARM setting.

3. Cut three circles from each tortilla with 2-inch biscuit cutter. Top each evenly with pork, cheese and sour cream. Serve warm.

MAKES 12 SERVINGS

TIP: Carnitas, or "little meats" in Spanish, are a festive way to spice up any gathering. Carnitas traditionally include a large amount of lard, but slow cooking makes the dish healthier by eliminating the need to add lard, oil or fat, while keeping the meat tender and delicious.

Thai Coconut Chicken Meatballs

1 pound ground chicken
2 green onions, chopped
1 clove garlic, minced
2 teaspoons toasted sesame oil
2 teaspoons mirin
1 teaspoon fish sauce
½ cup unsweetened canned coconut milk
¼ cup chicken broth
2 teaspoons packed brown sugar
1 teaspoon Thai red curry paste
1 tablespoon canola oil
2 teaspoons lime juice
2 tablespoons water
1 tablespoon cornstarch

1. Combine chicken, green onions, garlic, sesame oil, mirin and fish sauce in large bowl. Shape into 1½-inch meatballs. Combine coconut milk, broth, brown sugar and curry paste in small bowl.

2. Heat canola oil in large skillet over medium-high heat. Add meatballs in batches; cook and stir 3 to 5 minutes until browned on all sides. Remove to **CROCK-POT**® slow cooker. Add coconut milk mixture. Cover; cook on HIGH 3½ to 4 hours.

3. Stir in lime juice. Stir water into cornstarch in small bowl until smooth. Whisk into sauce in **CROCK-POT**® slow cooker. Cook, uncovered, on HIGH 10 to 15 minutes or until sauce is slightly thickened.

MAKES 4 TO 5 SERVINGS

TIP: Meatballs that are of equal size will be finished cooking at the same time. To ensure your meatballs are the same size, pat seasoned ground meat into an even rectangle and then slice into even rows and columns. Roll each portion into a smooth ball.

Warm Moroccan-Style Bean Dip

2 teaspoons canola oil

1 small onion, chopped

2 cloves garlic, minced

2 cans (about 15 ounces *each*) cannellini beans, rinsed and drained

¾ cup canned diced tomatoes, drained

½ teaspoon ground turmeric (optional)

¼ teaspoon salt

¼ teaspoon ground cinnamon

¼ teaspoon paprika

¼ teaspoon black pepper

¼ teaspoon ground cumin

⅛ teaspoon ground cloves

⅛ teaspoon ground red pepper

2 tablespoons plain yogurt

1 tablespoon cold water

¼ teaspoon dried mint (optional)

Warm pita bread rounds, cut into wedges

1. Heat oil in small skillet over medium-high heat. Add onion; cook 5 to 6 minutes or until translucent. Add garlic; cook 45 seconds. Remove to **CROCK-POT®** slow cooker. Stir in beans, tomatoes and spices. Cover; cook on LOW 6 hours.

2. Remove bean mixture and cooking liquid to food processor or blender; pulse to make coarse paste. Alternatively, use immersion blender to chop beans to coarse paste in **CROCK-POT®** slow cooker. Remove to large serving plate or bowl.

3. Beat yogurt and cold water together in small bowl until well combined. Drizzle over bean dip. Garnish with mint. Serve warm with pita wedges.

MAKES 4 TO 6 SERVINGS

TIP: Moroccan cuisine has a wide array of dishes beyond the most famous couscous. The cuisine makes use of a wide variety of spices; this reflects the many ethnicities that have influenced the country over the centuries. This spice-filled dip is sure to stimulate guests' taste buds.

Sweet and Spicy Sausage Rounds

1 pound kielbasa sausage, cut into ¼-inch-thick rounds

⅔ cup blackberry jam

⅓ cup steak sauce

1 tablespoon yellow mustard

½ teaspoon ground allspice

Combine sausage, jam, steak sauce, mustard and allspice in **CROCK-POT®** slow cooker; stir to blend. Cover; cook on HIGH 3 hours.

MAKES ABOUT 16 SERVINGS

Bacon-Wrapped Dates

4 ounces goat cheese or blue cheese

1 package (8 ounces) dried pitted dates

1 pound thick-cut bacon (about 11 slices), halved

1. Fill **CROCK-POT®** slow cooker with about ½-inch water. Spoon goat cheese evenly into centers of dates; close. Wrap half slice of bacon around each date; secure with toothpicks.

2. Heat large skillet over medium heat. Add wrapped dates; cook and turn 5 to 10 minutes until browned. Remove to **CROCK-POT®** slow cooker.

3. Cover; cook on LOW 2 to 3 hours. Remove toothpicks before serving.

MAKES 8 TO 10 SERVINGS

Sweet and Spicy Sausage Rounds

Spiced Beer Fondue

2 tablespoons butter

2 tablespoons all-purpose flour

1 can (8 ounces) light-colored beer, such as ale or lager

½ cup half-and-half

1 cup (4 ounces) shredded smoked gouda cheese

2 teaspoons coarse grain mustard

1 teaspoon Worcestershire sauce

⅛ teaspoon salt

⅛ teaspoon ground red pepper

Dash ground nutmeg (optional)

Apple slices and cooked potato wedges

1. Melt butter in medium saucepan over medium heat. Sprinkle with flour; whisk until smooth. Stir in beer and half-and-half; bring to a boil. Cook and stir 2 minutes. Stir in cheese, mustard, Worcestershire sauce, salt and ground red pepper; cook and stir until cheese is melted.

2. Coat inside of **CROCK-POT® LITTLE DIPPER®** slow cooker with nonstick cooking spray. Fill with warm fondue. Sprinkle with nutmeg, if desired, and serve with apples and potatoes.

MAKES 1½ CUPS

Chicken and Brie Sliders

1 red bell pepper, chopped

1 to 2 carrots, sliced

½ cup sliced celery

1 onion, chopped

1 clove garlic, minced

¼ teaspoon dried oregano

¼ teaspoon red pepper flakes

¼ cup all-purpose flour

1 teaspoon salt

½ teaspoon black pepper

6 boneless, skinless chicken thighs or breasts

1 tablespoon vegetable oil

1 can (about 14 ounces) chicken broth

6 sub rolls, split and toasted or 2 thin baguettes (about 12 ounces *each*), split and toasted

1 large wedge brie cheese, cut into 12 pieces

1. Place bell pepper, carrots, celery, onion, garlic, oregano and red pepper flakes in **CROCK-POT®** slow cooker.

2. Combine flour, salt and black pepper in large resealable food storage bag. Add chicken, two pieces at a time; shake to coat with flour mixture. Heat oil in large skillet over medium-high heat. Add chicken; cook 6 to 8 minutes or until browned on both sides.

3. Place chicken over vegetables in **CROCK-POT®** slow cooker; add broth. Cover; cook on LOW 5 to 6 hours.

4. Remove one piece of chicken from **CROCK-POT®** slow cooker, slice thinly and arrange on 1 sub roll. Spoon 1 to 2 tablespoons broth mixture over chicken and top with 2 slices cheese. Repeat with remaining chicken, bread and cheese. Slice each sandwich into three equal pieces.

MAKES 18 SLIDERS

Pancetta Horseradish Dip

3 slices pancetta

8 ounces cream cheese, cubed

¾ cup (3 ounces) shredded Swiss cheese

¼ cup whipping cream

¼ cup chopped green onions, plus additional for topping

1 tablespoon prepared horseradish, drained

1 teaspoon Worcestershire sauce

½ teaspoon Dijon mustard

Additional green onions (optional)

Potato chips

1. Heat small skillet over medium heat. Add pancetta; cook 4 minutes or until crisp, turning occasionally. Drain on paper towels. Let cool then crumble and set aside.

2. Coat inside of **CROCK-POT® LITTLE DIPPER®** slow cooker with nonstick cooking spray. Add cream cheese, Swiss cheese, whipping cream, ¼ cup green onions, horseradish, Worcestershire sauce and mustard. Cover; heat 1 hour then stir. Cover; heat 30 minutes or until cheese is melted.

3. Stir in all but 2 teaspoons pancetta. Sprinkle remaining pancetta and additional green onions on top. Serve with potato chips.

MAKES ABOUT 1½ CUPS

Chesapeake Bay Crab Dip

1 can (6½ ounces) crabmeat, well drained

3 ounces cream cheese, cubed

⅓ cup sour cream

3 tablespoons mayonnaise

2 tablespoons finely chopped onion

½ teaspoon Chesapeake Bay seasoning

¼ teaspoon hot pepper sauce

1 tablespoon chopped fresh chives

Multi-grain crackers

Baby carrots

1. Coat inside of **CROCK-POT® LITTLE DIPPER®** slow cooker. Pick out and discard any shell or cartilage from crabmeat. Add crabmeat, cream cheese, sour cream, mayonnaise, onion, Chesapeake Bay seasoning and hot pepper sauce; stir until blended.

2. Cover; heat 1 hour. Stir well. Cover; heat 30 minutes. Stir in chives. Serve with crackers and carrots.

MAKES ABOUT 1½ CUPS

Party Meatballs

1 package (about 1 pound) frozen cocktail-size turkey or beef meatballs
½ cup maple syrup
1 jar (12 ounces) chili sauce
1 jar (12 ounces) grape jelly

Place meatballs, syrup, chili sauce and jelly in **CROCK-POT**® slow cooker; stir to blend. Cover; cook on LOW 3 to 4 hours or on HIGH 2 to 3 hours.

MAKES 10 TO 12 SERVINGS

Nacho Dip

1 tablespoon vegetable oil
1 onion, chopped
2 pounds ground beef
2 cans (about 15 ounces *each*) black beans, rinsed and drained
1 can (28 ounces) diced tomatoes
1 can (about 15 ounces) refried beans
1 can (about 15 ounces) cream-style corn
3 cloves garlic, minced
1 package (1 ounce) taco seasoning mix
Tortilla chips
Queso blanco

1. Heat oil in large skillet over medium-high heat. Add onion; cook 2 to 3 minutes or until translucent. Add beef; brown 6 to 8 minutes, stirring to break up meat. Drain fat.

2. Stir beef mixture, black beans, tomatoes, refried beans, corn, garlic and taco seasoning mix into **CROCK-POT**® slow cooker. Cover; cook on LOW 5 to 6 hours or on HIGH 2½ to 3 hours. Serve on tortilla chips. Sprinkle with queso blanco.

MAKES 10 CUPS

Party Meatballs

Creamy Artichoke-Parmesan Dip

1 teaspoon olive oil

2 tablespoons finely chopped onion

½ can (about 7 ounces) artichoke hearts, drained and chopped

½ cup half-and-half

½ cup (2 ounces) mozzarella cheese

⅓ cup grated Parmesan cheese

⅓ cup mayonnaise

⅛ teaspoon dried oregano

⅛ teaspoon garlic powder

4 pita bread rounds, toasted and cut into wedges

Fresh vegetables

1. Heat oil in medium saucepan over medium heat. Add onion; cook and stir 3 to 5 minutes or until tender. Add artichoke hearts, half-and-half, cheeses, mayonnaise, oregano and garlic powder; cook and stir 5 to 7 minutes or until mixture comes to a boil.

2. Coat inside of **CROCK-POT® LITTLE DIPPER®** slow cooker with nonstick cooking spray. Fill with warm dip. Serve with pita wedges and vegetables.

MAKES 1½ CUPS

Soups, Stews and Chilies

Chicken and Vegetable Soup

1 tablespoon olive oil

2 medium parsnips, cut into ½-inch pieces

2 medium carrots, cut into ½-inch pieces

2 medium onions, chopped

2 stalks celery, cut into ½-inch pieces

1 whole chicken (3 to 3½ pounds)

4 cups chicken broth

10 sprigs fresh Italian parsley *or* 1½ teaspoons dried parsley flakes

4 sprigs fresh thyme *or* ½ teaspoon dried thyme

1. Coat inside of **CROCK-POT**® slow cooker with nonstick cooking spray. Heat oil in large skillet over medium-high heat. Add parsnips, carrots, onions and celery; cook and stir 5 minutes or until vegetables are softened. Remove parsnip mixture to **CROCK-POT**® slow cooker. Add chicken, broth, parsley and thyme.

2. Cover; cook on LOW 6 to 7 hours. Remove chicken to large cutting board; let stand 10 minutes. Remove and discard skin and bones from chicken. Shred chicken using two forks. Stir shredded chicken into **CROCK-POT**® slow cooker.

MAKES 10 SERVINGS

Pozole Rojo

4 dried ancho chiles, stemmed and seeded

3 dried guajillo chiles, stemmed and seeded*

2 cups boiling water

2½ pounds boneless pork shoulder, trimmed and cut in half

3 teaspoons salt, divided

1 tablespoon vegetable oil

2 medium onions, chopped

1½ tablespoons minced garlic

2 teaspoons ground cumin

2 teaspoons Mexican oregano**

4 cups chicken broth

2 cans (30 ounces *each*) white hominy, rinsed and drained

Sliced radishes (optional)

Guajillo chiles can be found in the ethnic section of most large supermarkets.

**Mexican oregano has a much stronger flavor than regular oregano.*

1. Place ancho and guajillo chiles in medium bowl; pour boiling water over top. Weigh down chiles with small plate or bowl; soak 30 minutes.

2. Meanwhile, season pork with 1 teaspoon salt. Heat oil in large skillet over medium-high heat. Add pork; cook 8 to 10 minutes or until browned on all sides. Remove to **CROCK-POT®** slow cooker.

3. Heat same skillet over medium heat. Add onions; cook 6 minutes or until softened. Add garlic, cumin, oregano and remaining 2 teaspoons salt; cook and stir 1 minute. Stir in broth; bring to a simmer, scraping up any browned bits from bottom of skillet. Pour over pork in **CROCK-POT®** slow cooker.

4. Place softened chiles and soaking liquid in food processor or blender; blend until smooth. Pour through fine-mesh sieve into medium bowl, pressing with spoon to extract liquids. Discard solids. Stir mixture into **CROCK-POT®** slow cooker.

5. Cover; cook on LOW 5 hours. Stir in hominy. Cover; cook on LOW 1 hour. Turn off heat. Let stand 10 to 15 minutes. Skim off fat and discard. Remove pork to large cutting board; shred with two forks. Ladle hominy mixture into bowls; top each serving with pork and sliced radishes, if desired.

MAKES 8 SERVINGS

Broccoli Cheddar Soup

3 tablespoons butter

1 medium onion, chopped

3 tablespoons all-purpose flour

¼ teaspoon ground nutmeg

¼ teaspoon black pepper

4 cups vegetable broth

1 large bunch broccoli, chopped

1 medium red potato, peeled and chopped

1 teaspoon salt

1 whole bay leaf

1½ cups (6 ounces) shredded Cheddar cheese, plus additional for garnish

½ cup whipping cream

1. Melt butter in medium saucepan over medium heat. Add onion; cook and stir 6 minutes or until softened. Add flour, nutmeg and pepper; cook and stir 1 minute. Remove to **CROCK-POT**® slow cooker. Stir in broth, broccoli, potato, salt and bay leaf.

2. Cover; cook on HIGH 3 hours. Remove and discard bay leaf. Add soup in batches to food processor or blender; purée until desired consistency. Pour soup back into **CROCK-POT**® slow cooker. Stir in 1½ cups cheese and cream until cheese is melted. Garnish with additional cheese.

MAKES 6 SERVINGS

Shrimp and Okra Gumbo

1 tablespoon olive oil

8 ounces kielbasa, halved lengthwise and cut into 1/4-inch-thick half moons

1 green bell pepper, chopped

1 medium onion, chopped

3 stalks celery, cut into 1/4-inch slices

6 green onions, chopped

4 cloves garlic, minced

1 cup chicken broth

1 can (about 14 ounces) diced tomatoes

1 teaspoon Cajun seasoning

1/2 teaspoon dried thyme

1 pound large shrimp, peeled and deveined (with tails on)

2 cups frozen cut okra, thawed

1. Coat inside of **CROCK-POT**® slow cooker with nonstick cooking spray. Heat oil in large skillet over medium-high heat. Add kielbasa; cook and stir 4 minutes until browned. Remove to **CROCK-POT**® slow cooker.

2. Return skillet to medium-high heat. Add bell pepper, chopped onion, celery, green onions and garlic; cook and stir 5 to 6 minutes until vegetables are crisp-tender. Remove to **CROCK-POT**® slow cooker. Stir in broth, tomatoes, Cajun seasoning and thyme.

3. Cover; cook on LOW 4 hours. Stir in shrimp and okra. Cover; cook on LOW 1 hour.

MAKES 6 SERVINGS

Turkey Chili

2 tablespoons olive oil, divided
1½ pounds ground turkey
2 medium onions, chopped
1 medium red bell pepper, chopped
1 medium green bell pepper, chopped
5 cloves garlic, minced
1 jalapeño pepper, finely chopped*

2 cans (about 14 ounces *each*) fire-roasted diced tomatoes
4 teaspoons chili powder
1 teaspoon ground cumin
1 teaspoon dried oregano
½ teaspoon salt

*Jalapeño peppers can sting and irritate the skin, so wear rubber gloves when handling peppers and do not touch your eyes.

1. Heat 1 tablespoon oil in large skillet over medium-high heat. Add turkey; cook 7 to 8 minutes, stirring to break up meat. Remove to **CROCK-POT®** slow cooker.

2. Heat remaining 1 tablespoon oil in same skillet over medium-high heat. Add onions, bell peppers, garlic and jalapeño pepper; cook and stir 4 to 5 minutes or until softened. Stir in tomatoes, chili powder, cumin, oregano and salt; cook 1 minute. Remove onion mixture to **CROCK-POT®** slow cooker. Cover; cook on LOW 6 hours.

MAKES 6 SERVINGS

Beef and Beet Borscht

6 slices bacon

1 boneless beef chuck roast (1½ pounds), trimmed and cut into ½-inch pieces

1 medium onion, chopped

4 cloves garlic, minced

4 medium beets, peeled and cut into ½-inch pieces

2 large carrots, sliced

3 cups beef broth

6 sprigs fresh dill

3 tablespoons honey

3 tablespoons red wine vinegar

2 whole bay leaves

3 cups shredded green cabbage

1. Heat large skillet over medium heat. Add bacon; cook and stir until crisp. Remove to paper-towel lined plate using slotted spoon; crumble.

2. Return skillet to medium-high heat. Add beef; cook 5 minutes or until browned. Remove beef to **CROCK-POT®** slow cooker.

3. Pour off all but 1 tablespoon fat from skillet. Add onion and garlic; cook 4 minutes or until onion is softened. Remove onion mixture to **CROCK-POT®** slow cooker. Stir in beets, carrots, broth, bacon, dill, honey, vinegar and bay leaves.

4. Cover; cook on LOW 5 to 6 hours. Stir in cabbage. Cover; cook on LOW 30 minutes. Remove and discard bay leaves before serving.

MAKES 6 TO 8 SERVINGS

Seafood Cioppino

1 tablespoon olive oil
1 medium fennel bulb, thinly sliced
1 medium onion, chopped
4 cloves garlic, minced
1 teaspoon dried basil
¼ teaspoon saffron threads, crushed (optional)
1 can (about 14 ounces) diced tomatoes

1 (8-ounce) bottle clam juice
16 little neck clams, scrubbed
24 mussels, scrubbed
1 pound cod fillet, cut into 8 pieces
8 ounces large shrimp, peeled and deveined (with tails on)
½ teaspoon salt
⅛ teaspoon black pepper

1. Coat inside of **CROCK-POT**® slow cooker with nonstick cooking spray. Heat oil in large skillet over medium-high heat. Add fennel, onion, garlic, basil and saffron, if desired; cook and stir 4 to 5 minutes or until vegetables are softened. Remove onion mixture to **CROCK-POT**® slow cooker. Stir in tomatoes and clam juice.

2. Cover; cook on HIGH 2 to 3 hours. Add clams. Cover; cook on HIGH 30 minutes. Add mussels. Cover; cook on HIGH 15 minutes.

3. Season cod and shrimp with salt and pepper. Place on top of shellfish. Cover; cook on HIGH 25 to 30 minutes until clams and mussels have opened and fish is cooked through.

MAKES 4 SERVINGS

White Chicken Chili

8 ounces dried navy beans, rinsed and sorted

1 tablespoon vegetable oil

2 pounds boneless, skinless chicken breasts (about 4)

2 onions, chopped

1 tablespoon minced garlic

2 teaspoons ground cumin

2 teaspoons salt

1 teaspoon dried oregano

¼ teaspoon black pepper

¼ teaspoon ground red pepper (optional)

4 cups chicken broth

1 can (4 ounces) fire-roasted diced green chiles, rinsed and drained

¼ cup chopped fresh cilantro

Tortilla chips (optional)

Lime wedges (optional)

1. Place beans on bottom of **CROCK-POT**® slow cooker. Heat oil in large skillet over medium-high heat. Add chicken; cook 8 minutes or until browned on all sides. Remove to **CROCK-POT**® slow cooker.

2. Heat same skillet over medium heat. Add onions; cook 6 minutes or until softened and lightly browned. Add garlic, cumin, salt, oregano, black pepper and ground red pepper, if desired; cook and stir 1 minute. Add broth; bring to a simmer, stirring to scrape up any browned bits from bottom of skillet. Remove onion mixture to **CROCK-POT**® slow cooker.

3. Cover; cook on LOW 5 hours. Remove chicken to large cutting board; shred with two forks. Return chicken to **CROCK-POT**® slow cooker. Stir in cilantro. Serve with tortilla chips and lime wedges, if desired.

MAKES 6 TO 8 SERVINGS

Hearty Pork and Bacon Chili

2½ pounds pork shoulder, cut into 1-inch pieces

3½ teaspoons salt, divided

1¼ teaspoons black pepper, divided

1 tablespoon vegetable oil

4 slices thick-cut bacon, diced

2 medium onions, chopped

1 red bell pepper, chopped

¼ cup chili powder

2 tablespoons tomato paste

1 tablespoon minced garlic

1 tablespoon ground cumin

1 tablespoon smoked paprika

1 bottle (12 ounces) pale ale

2 cans (about 14 ounces *each*) diced tomatoes

2 cups water

¾ cup dried kidney beans, rinsed and sorted

¾ cup dried black beans, rinsed and sorted

3 tablespoons cornmeal

Chopped fresh cilantro leaves and feta cheese (optional)

1. Season pork with 1 teaspoon salt and 1 teaspoon black pepper. Heat oil in large skillet over medium-high heat. Cook pork in batches 6 minutes or until browned on all sides. Remove to **CROCK-POT**® slow cooker using slotted spoon.

2. Heat same skillet over medium heat. Add bacon; cook 6 minutes or until crisp, stirring occasionally. Remove to **CROCK-POT**® slow cooker using slotted spoon.

3. Pour off all but 2 tablespoons fat from skillet. Return skillet to medium heat. Add onions and bell pepper; cook and stir 6 minutes or just until softened. Stir in chili powder, tomato paste, garlic, cumin, smoked paprika, remaining 2½ teaspoons salt and ¼ teaspoon black pepper; cook and stir 1 minute. Stir in ale. Bring to a simmer, scraping up any browned bits from bottom of skillet. Pour over pork in **CROCK-POT**® slow cooker. Stir in tomatoes, water, beans and cornmeal.

4. Cover; cook on LOW 10 hours. Turn off heat. Let stand 10 minutes. Skim off and discard fat. Garnish each serving with cilantro and cheese.

MAKES 8 TO 10 SERVINGS

Three-Bean Chili with Chorizo

2 Mexican chorizo sausages (about 6 ounces *each*), casings removed

1 tablespoon vegetable oil

1 large onion, chopped

1 tablespoon salt

1 tablespoon tomato paste

1 tablespoon minced garlic

1 tablespoon chili powder

1 tablespoon ancho chili powder

2 to 3 teaspoons chipotle chili powder

2 teaspoons ground cumin

1 teaspoon ground coriander

3 cups water

2 cans (about 14 ounces *each*) crushed tomatoes

½ cup dried pinto beans, rinsed and sorted

½ cup dried kidney beans, rinsed and sorted

½ cup dried black beans, rinsed and sorted

Optional toppings: sour cream, green onions and/or chopped fresh cilantro

1. Heat large nonstick skillet over medium-high heat. Add sausage; cook 3 to 4 minutes, stirring to break up meat. Remove to **CROCK-POT**® slow cooker using slotted spoon.

2. Wipe out skillet. Heat oil in same skillet over medium heat. Add onion; cook and stir 6 minutes or until softened. Add salt, tomato paste, garlic, chili powders, cumin and coriander; cook and stir 1 minute. Remove to **CROCK-POT**® slow cooker. Stir in water, tomatoes and beans.

3. Cover; cook on LOW 10 hours. Serve with desired toppings.

MAKES 6 TO 8 SERVINGS

NOTE: For spicier chili, use 1 tablespoon chipotle chili powder.

Lamb and Chickpea Stew

1 pound lamb stew meat

2 teaspoons salt, divided

2 tablespoons vegetable oil, divided

1 large onion, chopped

1 tablespoon minced garlic

1½ teaspoons ground cumin

1 teaspoon ground turmeric

1 teaspoon ground coriander

1 teaspoon ground cinnamon

¼ teaspoon black pepper

2 cups chicken broth

1 cup diced canned tomatoes, drained

1 cup dried chickpeas, rinsed and sorted

½ cup chopped dried apricots

¼ cup chopped fresh Italian parsley

2 tablespoons honey

2 tablespoons lemon juice

Hot cooked couscous

1. Season lamb with ½ teaspoon salt. Heat 1 tablespoon oil in large skillet over medium-high heat. Add lamb; cook 8 minutes or until browned on all sides. Remove to **CROCK-POT**® slow cooker.

2. Heat remaining 1 tablespoon oil in same skillet over medium heat. Add onion; cook and stir 6 minutes or until softened. Add garlic, remaining 1½ teaspoons salt, cumin, turmeric, coriander, cinnamon and pepper; cook and stir 1 minute. Add broth and tomatoes; cook and stir 5 minutes, scraping up any brown bits from bottom of skillet. Remove to **CROCK-POT**® slow cooker. Stir in chickpeas.

3. Cover; cook on LOW 7 hours. Stir in apricots. Cover; cook on LOW 1 hour. Turn off heat. Let stand 10 minutes. Skim off and discard fat. Stir in parsley, honey and lemon juice. Serve over couscous.

MAKES 6 SERVINGS

Texas Chili

3½ to 4 pounds cubed beef stew meat
  Salt and black pepper
4 tablespoons vegetable oil, divided
1 large onion, diced
¼ cup chili powder
1 tablespoon minced garlic
1 tablespoon ground cumin
1 tablespoon tomato paste

2 teaspoons ground coriander
1 teaspoon dried oregano
3 cans (about 14 ounces *each*) diced tomatoes
3 tablespoons cornmeal or masa harina
1 tablespoon packed light brown sugar
  Cornbread (optional)

1. Season beef with salt and pepper. Heat 3 tablespoons oil in large skillet over medium-high heat. Cook beef in batches 8 minutes or until browned on all sides. Remove to **CROCK-POT®** slow cooker.

2. Heat remaining 1 tablespoon oil in same skillet. Add onion; cook and stir 6 minutes or until softened. Stir in chili powder, garlic, cumin, tomato paste, coriander, oregano, and additional salt and pepper, as desired; cook and stir 1 minute. Stir in tomatoes, cornmeal and brown sugar; bring to a simmer. Remove to **CROCK-POT®** slow cooker.

3. Cover; cook on LOW 7 to 8 hours. Serve with cornbread, if desired.

MAKES 8 SERVINGS

VARIATION: Add ¼ teaspoon ground red pepper if a spicier chili is desired.

Soups, Stews and Chilies

Chicken and Mushroom Stew

4 tablespoons vegetable oil, divided

2 medium leeks, white and light green parts only, halved lengthwise and thinly sliced crosswise

1 carrot, cut into 1-inch pieces

1 stalk celery, diced

6 boneless, skinless chicken thighs (about 2 pounds)

Salt and black pepper

12 ounces cremini mushrooms, quartered

¼ cup all-purpose flour

1 ounce dried porcini mushrooms, rehydrated in 1½ cups hot water and chopped, soaking liquid strained and reserved

1 teaspoon minced garlic

1 sprig fresh thyme

1 whole bay leaf

½ cup dry white wine

1 cup chicken broth

1. Heat 1 tablespoon oil in large skillet over medium heat. Add leeks; cook 8 minutes or until softened. Remove to **CROCK-POT**® slow cooker. Add carrot and celery.

2. Heat 1 tablespoon oil in same skillet over medium-high heat. Season chicken with salt and pepper. Add chicken in batches; cook 8 minutes or until browned on both sides. Remove to **CROCK-POT**® slow cooker.

3. Heat remaining 2 tablespoons oil in same skillet. Add cremini mushrooms; cook 7 minutes or until mushrooms have released their liquid and started to brown. Add flour, porcini mushrooms, garlic, thyme and bay leaf; cook and stir 1 minute. Add wine; cook until evaporated, stirring to scrape any browned bits from bottom of skillet. Add reserved soaking liquid and broth; bring to a simmer. Pour mixture into **CROCK-POT**® slow cooker.

4. Cover; cook on HIGH 2 to 3 hours. Remove thyme sprig and bay leaf before serving.

MAKES 6 SERVINGS

Hearty Sausage and Tortellini Soup

3 hot Italian sausages, casings removed

3 sweet Italian sausages, casings removed

5 cups chicken broth

1 can (about 14 ounces) diced tomatoes with garlic and oregano

1 can (about 8 ounces) tomato sauce

1 large onion, chopped

2 medium carrots, chopped

1 teaspoon seasoned salt

½ teaspoon Italian seasoning

¼ teaspoon black pepper

1 package (9 ounces) refrigerated cheese tortellini

1 medium zucchini, chopped

2 cups broccoli, chopped

1. Cook sausages in large skillet over medium-high heat 8 to 10 minutes. Drain fat. Add sausages, broth, diced tomatoes, tomato sauce, onion, carrots, seasoned salt, Italian seasoning and pepper to **CROCK-POT**® slow cooker. Cover; cook on LOW 6 to 8 hours or on HIGH 3 to 4 hours.

2. Meanwhile, cook tortellini according to package directions. Add tortellini, zucchini and broccoli to **CROCK-POT**® slow cooker during last 15 to 20 minutes of cooking.

MAKES 6 TO 8 SERVINGS

Soups, Stews and Chilies

Chicken Orzo Soup

1 tablespoon vegetable oil

1 onion, diced

1 fennel bulb, quartered, cored, thinly sliced, tops removed and fronds reserved for garnish

2 teaspoons minced garlic

8 cups chicken broth

2 boneless, skinless chicken breasts (8 ounces *each*)

2 carrots, peeled and thinly sliced

2 sprigs fresh thyme

1 whole bay leaf

Salt and black pepper

½ cup uncooked orzo

Oyster crackers (optional)

1. Heat oil in large skillet over medium heat. Add onion and fennel; cook 8 minutes or until tender. Add garlic; cook and stir 1 minute. Remove to **CROCK-POT**® slow cooker. Add broth, chicken, carrots, thyme and bay leaf. Season with salt and pepper. Cover; cook on HIGH 2 to 3 hours.

2. Remove chicken to large cutting board; shred with two forks. Add orzo to **CROCK-POT**® slow cooker. Cover; cook on HIGH 30 minutes. Stir shredded chicken into **CROCK-POT**® slow cooker. Remove and discard bay thyme sprigs and bay leaf. Garnish each serving with reserved fennel fronds. Serve with crackers, if desired.

MAKES 6 TO 8 SERVINGS

Italian Wedding Soup
with Three-Cheese Tortellini

6 cups chicken broth

2½ cups kale, stemmed and chopped

1 package (16 ounces) frozen Italian-style meatballs

1 package (9 ounces) refrigerated three-cheese tortellini

1 cup celery, chopped

1 small onion, thinly sliced

1 teaspoon dried basil

Juice of 1 lemon

1 tablespoon minced garlic

⅛ teaspoon salt

⅛ teaspoon sugar

Black pepper

Combine broth, kale, meatballs, tortellini, celery, onion, basil, lemon juice, garlic, salt, sugar and pepper in **CROCK-POT**® slow cooker. Cover; cook on LOW 3 to 4 hours, stirring halfway through cooking time.

MAKES 8 SERVINGS

Fall Harvest Stew

2½ pounds cubed beef stew meat

¼ cup all-purpose flour

2 tablespoons olive oil

1 tablespoon butter

1 medium onion, chopped

1 head garlic, minced

2 whole bay leaves

1 tablespoon fresh rosemary, chopped

1½ teaspoons fresh thyme, chopped

½ cup beef broth, divided

1 pound carrots, cut into 2-inch pieces

4 turnips, cut into 1-inch pieces

1 butternut squash, cut into 2-inch pieces

1 can (12 ounces) stout, divided

⅛ teaspoon white pepper

Dash apple pie spice

Salt and black pepper

1. Place beef and flour in large bowl; toss to coat beef. Heat oil and butter in large skillet over medium-high heat. Add beef; cook and stir 6 to 8 minutes or until browned on all sides. Remove to **CROCK-POT®** slow cooker.

2. Return skillet to heat. Add onion, garlic, bay leaves, rosemary and thyme; cook until onion begins to soften. Add mixture to **CROCK-POT®** slow cooker.

3. Return skillet to heat. Add ¼ cup broth, stirring to scrape up any browned bits from bottom of skillet. Add broth mixture, carrots, turnips, squash, stout, white pepper and apple pie spice to **CROCK-POT®** slow cooker. Season with salt and black pepper. Add remaining ¼ cup broth. Cover; cook on LOW 8 hours. Remove and discard bay leaves.

MAKES 8 SERVINGS

Jamaican Quinoa and Sweet Potato Stew

3 cups vegetable broth

1 large or 2 small sweet potatoes (12 ounces), cut into ¾-inch pieces

1 cup uncooked quinoa, rinsed and drained

1 large red bell pepper, cut into ¾-inch pieces

1 tablespoon Caribbean jerk seasoning

¼ cup chopped fresh cilantro

¼ cup sliced almonds, toasted*

Hot pepper sauce or Pickapeppa sauce (optional)

To toast almonds, spread in single layer in heavy skillet. Cook over medium heat 1 to 2 minutes or until nuts are lightly browned, stirring frequently.

1. Coat inside of **CROCK-POT**® slow cooker with nonstick cooking spray. Combine broth, sweet potatoes, quinoa, bell pepper and jerk seasoning in **CROCK-POT**® slow cooker. Cover; cook on LOW 5 to 6 hours or on HIGH 2 to 2½ hours or until vegetables are tender.

2. Ladle into shallow bowls; top with cilantro and almonds. Serve with hot pepper sauce.

MAKES 4 SERVINGS

Wild Mushroom Beef Stew

1½ to 2 pounds cubed beef stew meat
2 tablespoons all-purpose flour
½ teaspoon salt
½ teaspoon black pepper
1½ cups beef broth
4 shiitake mushrooms, sliced
2 medium potatoes, diced

2 medium carrots, sliced
1 small white onion, chopped
1 stalk celery, sliced
1 teaspoon paprika
1 clove garlic, minced
1 teaspoon Worcestershire sauce
1 whole bay leaf

Place beef in **CROCK-POT**® slow cooker. Combine flour, salt and pepper in small bowl; stir to blend. Sprinkle flour mixture over meat; toss to coat. Add broth, mushrooms, potatoes, carrots, onion, celery, paprika, garlic, Worcestershire sauce and bay leaf; stir to blend. Cover; cook on LOW 10 to 12 hours or on HIGH 4 to 6 hours. Remove and discard bay leaf.

MAKES 5 SERVINGS

NOTE: This classic beef stew is given a twist with the addition of flavorful shiitake mushrooms. If shiitake mushrooms are unavailable in your local grocery store, you can substitute other mushrooms of your choice. For extra punch, add a few dried porcini mushrooms.

TIP: You may double the amount of meat, mushrooms, carrots, potatoes, onion and celery for a 5-, 6- or 7-quart **CROCK-POT**® slow cooker.

Cauliflower Soup

2 heads cauliflower, cut into small florets
8 cups chicken broth
¾ cup chopped celery
¾ cup chopped onion
2 teaspoons salt
2 teaspoons black pepper
2 cups milk or light cream
1 teaspoon Worcestershire sauce

1. Combine cauliflower, broth, celery, onion, salt and pepper in **CROCK-POT®** slow cooker; stir to blend. Cover; cook on LOW 7 to 8 hours or on HIGH 3 to 4 hours.

2. Pour cauliflower mixture into food processor or blender; process until smooth. Add milk and Worcestershire sauce; process until blended. Pour soup back into **CROCK-POT®** slow cooker. Cover; cook on HIGH 15 to 20 minutes or until heated through.

MAKES 8 SERVINGS

Pork Tenderloin Chili

1½ to 2 pounds pork tenderloin, cooked and cut into 2-inch pieces
2 cans (about 15 ounces *each*) pinto beans, rinsed and drained
2 cans (about 15 ounces *each*) black beans, rinsed and drained
2 cans (about 14 ounces *each*) whole tomatoes
2 cans (4 ounces *each*) diced mild green chiles
1 package taco seasoning mix
   Optional toppings: diced avocado, shredded cheese, chopped onion, cilantro and/or tortilla chips

Combine pork, beans, tomatoes, chiles and taco seasoning mix in **CROCK-POT®** slow cooker. Cover; cook on LOW 4 hours. Top as desired.

MAKES 8 SERVINGS

Cauliflower Soup

Cape Cod Stew

2 pounds medium raw shrimp, peeled and deveined

2 pounds fresh cod or other white fish

3 lobsters (1½ to 2½ pounds *each*), uncooked

1 pound mussels or clams

4 cups beef broth

2 cans (about 14 ounces *each*) chopped tomatoes

½ cup chopped onions

½ cup chopped carrots

½ cup chopped fresh cilantro

2 tablespoons sea salt

2 teaspoons crushed or minced garlic

2 teaspoons lemon juice

4 whole bay leaves

1 teaspoon dried thyme

½ teaspoon saffron threads

1. Cut shrimp and fish into bite-size pieces and place in large bowl; refrigerate. Remove lobster tails and claws. Chop tail into 2-inch pieces and separate claws at joints. Place lobster and mussels in large bowl; refrigerate.

2. Combine broth, tomatoes, onions, carrots, cilantro, salt, garlic, lemon juice, bay leaves, thyme and saffron in **CROCK-POT®** slow cooker. Cover; cook on LOW 7 hours.

3. Add seafood. Turn **CROCK-POT®** slow cooker to HIGH. Cover; cook on HIGH 45 minutes to 1 hour or until seafood is just cooked through. Remove and discard bay leaves. Discard any mussels that do not open.

MAKES 8 SERVINGS

Asian Sugar Snap Pea Soup

2 tablespoons peanut or canola oil

4 to 5 new potatoes, coarsely chopped

2 green onions, chopped

1 medium carrot, thinly sliced

1 stalk celery, thinly sliced

1 leek, thinly sliced

5 cups water

2 cups broccoli, cut into florets

1 tablespoon lemon juice

1 tablespoon soy sauce

1 teaspoon ground coriander

1 teaspoon ground cumin

1 teaspoon prepared horseradish

⅛ teaspoon ground red pepper

1 cup fresh sugar snap peas, rinsed and drained

4 cups cooked brown rice

1. Heat oil in large skillet over medium heat. Add potatoes, green onions, carrot, celery and leek; cook and stir 10 to 12 minutes or until vegetables begin to soften. Remove to **CROCK-POT**® slow cooker.

2. Add water, broccoli, lemon juice, soy sauce, coriander, cumin, horseradish and ground red pepper. Cover; cook on LOW 5 to 6 hours or on HIGH 2 to 3 hours.

3. Stir in peas. Cover; cook on HIGH 15 minutes or until peas are crisp-tender. To serve, portion rice into four bowls. Ladle soup over rice.

MAKES 4 SERVINGS

Pasta Fagioli Soup

2 cans (about 14 ounces *each*) beef or vegetable broth

1 can (about 15 ounces) Great Northern beans, rinsed and drained

1 can (about 14 ounces) diced tomatoes

2 zucchini, quartered lengthwise and sliced

1 tablespoon olive oil

1½ teaspoons minced garlic

½ teaspoon dried basil

½ teaspoon dried oregano

½ cup uncooked ditalini, tubetti or small shell pasta

½ cup garlic-seasoned croutons

½ cup grated Asiago or Romano cheese

3 tablespoons chopped fresh basil or Italian parsley (optional)

1. Combine broth, beans, tomatoes, zucchini, oil, garlic, dried basil and oregano in **CROCK-POT**® slow cooker; stir to blend. Cover; cook on LOW 3 to 4 hours.

2. Stir in pasta. Cover; cook on LOW 1 hour or until pasta is tender. Serve soup with croutons and cheese. Garnish with fresh basil.

MAKES 5 TO 6 SERVINGS

TIP: Only small pasta varieties like ditalini or tubetti pasta should be used in this recipe. The low heat of a **CROCK-POT**® slow cooker will not allow larger pasta shapes to cook completely.

French Onion Soup

¼ cup (½ stick) butter

3 pounds yellow onions, sliced

1 tablespoon sugar

2 to 3 tablespoons dry white wine

8 cups beef broth

8 to 16 slices French bread (optional)

½ cup (2 ounces) shredded Gruyère or Swiss cheese

1. Melt butter in large skillet over medium-low heat. Add onions; cover and cook 10 minutes or until onions are tender, but not browned.

2. Remove cover. Sprinkle sugar over onions. Cook and stir 8 to 10 minutes or until onions are caramelized. Add onions and any browned bits to **CROCK-POT®** slow cooker. Add wine to skillet. Bring to a boil, scraping up any browned bits from bottom of skillet. Add to **CROCK-POT®** slow cooker. Stir in broth. Cover; cook on LOW 8 hours or on HIGH 6 hours.

3. Preheat broiler. To serve, ladle soup into individual soup bowls. If desired, top each with 1 or 2 bread slices and about 1 tablespoon cheese. Place under broiler until cheese is melted and bubbly.

MAKES 8 SERVINGS

VARIATION: Substitute 1 cup dry white wine for 1 cup of beef broth.

What's for Dinner?

Miso-Poached Salmon

1½ cups water

2 green onions, cut into 2-inch-long pieces, plus additional for garnish

¼ cup yellow miso paste

¼ cup soy sauce

2 tablespoons sake

2 tablespoons mirin

1½ teaspoons grated fresh ginger

1 teaspoon minced garlic

6 salmon fillets (4 ounces *each*)

Hot cooked rice

1. Combine water, 2 green onions, miso paste, soy sauce, sake, mirin, ginger and garlic in **CROCK-POT**® slow cooker; stir to blend. Cover; cook on HIGH 30 minutes.

2. Turn **CROCK-POT**® slow cooker to LOW. Add salmon, skin side down. Cover; cook on LOW 30 minutes to 1 hour or until salmon turns opaque and flakes easily with a fork. Serve over rice with cooking liquid as desired. Garnish with additional green onions.

MAKES 6 SERVINGS

Black Bean, Zucchini and Corn Enchiladas

1 tablespoon vegetable oil
1 medium onion, chopped
2 medium zucchini, diced
2 cups corn
1 large red bell pepper, chopped
1 teaspoon minced garlic
½ teaspoon salt
½ teaspoon ground cumin

¼ teaspoon ground coriander
1 can (about 14 ounces) black beans, rinsed and drained
2 jars (16 ounces *each*) salsa verde
12 (6-inch) corn tortillas
2½ cups (10 ounces) shredded Monterey Jack cheese
2 tablespoons chopped fresh cilantro

1. Heat oil in large skillet over medium heat. Add onion; cook and stir 6 minutes or until softened. Add zucchini, corn and bell pepper; cook and stir 2 minutes. Add garlic, salt, cumin and coriander; cook and stir 1 minute. Stir in beans. Remove from heat.

2. Pour 1 cup salsa in bottom of **CROCK-POT**® slow cooker. Arrange 3 tortillas in single layer, cutting the tortillas in half as needed to fit. Spread 2 cups vegetable mixture over tortillas; sprinkle with ½ cup cheese. Repeat layers twice. Layer with remaining 3 tortillas; top with 2 cups salsa. Sprinkle with remaining 1 cup cheese. Reserve any remaining filling for another use.

3. Cover; cook on HIGH 2 hours or until cheese is bubbly and edges are lightly browned. Sprinkle with cilantro. Let stand 10 minutes before serving.

MAKES 6 SERVINGS

Maple-Dry Rubbed Ribs

2 teaspoons chili powder, divided
1 teaspoon ground coriander
1 teaspoon garlic powder, divided
½ teaspoon salt
¼ teaspoon black pepper

3 to 3½ pounds pork baby back ribs, trimmed and cut in half
3 tablespoons maple syrup, divided
1 can (about 8 ounces) tomato sauce
¼ teaspoon ground cinnamon
¼ teaspoon ground ginger

1. Coat inside of **CROCK-POT**® slow cooker with nonstick cooking spray. Combine 1 teaspoon chili powder, coriander, ½ teaspoon garlic powder, salt and pepper in small bowl; stir to blend. Brush ribs with 1 tablespoon syrup; rub with spice mixture. Place ribs into **CROCK-POT**® slow cooker.

2. Combine tomato sauce, remaining 1 teaspoon chili powder, remaining ½ teaspoon garlic powder, remaining 2 tablespoons syrup, cinnamon and ginger in medium bowl; stir to blend. Pour over ribs in **CROCK-POT**® slow cooker. Cover; cook on LOW 8 to 9 hours.

3. Turn off heat. Remove ribs to large serving platter; cover with foil to keep warm. Let sauce stand 5 to 10 minutes. Skim off and discard fat. Turn **CROCK-POT**® slow cooker to HIGH. Cook, partially covered, on HIGH 10 to 15 minutes or until sauce is thickened. Brush ribs with sauce and serve any remaining sauce on the side.

MAKES 4 SERVINGS

Chicken Meatballs in Spicy Tomato Sauce

3 tablespoons olive oil, divided	3 tablespoons tomato paste
1 medium onion, chopped	2 teaspoons salt, divided
6 cloves garlic, minced	1½ pounds ground chicken
1½ teaspoons dried basil	2 egg yolks
¼ teaspoon red pepper flakes	1 teaspoon dried oregano
2 cans (about 14 ounces *each*) diced tomatoes	¼ teaspoon black pepper
	Hot cooked pasta

1. Heat 2 tablespoons oil in large skillet over medium-high heat. Add onion, garlic, basil and red pepper flakes; cook and stir 5 minutes or until onion is softened. Remove half of mixture to **CROCK-POT®** slow cooker. Stir in diced tomatoes, tomato paste and 1 teaspoon salt.

2. Remove remaining onion mixture to large bowl. Add chicken, egg yolks, oregano, remaining 1 teaspoon salt and black pepper; mix well. Form mixture into 24 (1-inch) balls.

3. Heat remaining 1 tablespoon oil in large skillet. Add meatballs in batches; cook 7 minutes or until browned. Remove to **CROCK-POT®** slow cooker using slotted spoon. Cover; cook on LOW 4 to 5 hours. Serve over pasta.

MAKES 4 SERVINGS

Easy Salisbury Steak

1½ pounds ground beef
½ cup plain dry bread crumbs
1 egg
1 envelope onion soup mix*
1 can (10½ ounces) golden
   mushroom soup, undiluted

Hot cooked mashed potatoes
and asparagus (optional)

*You may pulse onion soup mix in a small
food processor or coffee grinder for a finer
grind, if desired.

1. Coat inside of **CROCK-POT**® slow cooker with nonstick cooking spray. Combine beef, bread crumbs, egg and onion soup mix in large bowl. Form mixture evenly into 4 (1-inch-thick) patties.

2. Heat large skillet over medium-high heat. Add patties; cook 2 minutes per side until lightly browned. Remove to **CROCK-POT**® slow cooker, in single layer. Spread mushroom soup evenly over patties. Cover; cook on LOW 3 to 3½ hours. Serve with potatoes and asparagus, if desired.

MAKES 4 SERVINGS

What's for Dinner?

Beef and Veal Meatloaf

1 tablespoon olive oil
1 small onion, chopped
½ red bell pepper, chopped
3 cloves garlic, minced
1 teaspoon dried oregano
1 pound ground beef

1 pound ground veal
1 egg
3 tablespoons tomato paste
1 teaspoon salt
½ teaspoon black pepper

1. Coat inside of **CROCK-POT**® slow cooker with nonstick cooking spray. Heat oil in large skillet over medium-high heat. Add onion, bell pepper, garlic and oregano; cook and stir 5 minutes until softened. Remove to large bowl; cool 6 minutes.

2. Add beef, veal, egg, tomato paste, salt and pepper to same large bowl; mix well. Form into 9×5-inch loaf; place in **CROCK-POT**® slow cooker. Cover; cook on LOW 5 to 6 hours. Remove meatloaf to large cutting board; let stand 10 minutes before slicing.

MAKES 6 SERVINGS

- cut up meat so all covered
- ? honey / thicker sauce

Pulled Pork with Honey-Chipotle Barbecue Sauce

3 teaspoons chili powder, divided

1 teaspoon chipotle chili powder, divided

1 teaspoon ground cumin, divided

1 teaspoon garlic powder, divided

1 teaspoon salt

3½ pounds bone-in pork shoulder, trimmed

1 can (15 ounces) tomato sauce

5 tablespoons honey, divided

Sweet potato chips and coleslaw (optional)

1. Coat inside of **CROCK-POT**® slow cooker with nonstick cooking spray. Combine 1 teaspoon chili powder, ½ teaspoon chipotle chili powder, ½ teaspoon cumin, ½ teaspoon garlic powder and salt in small bowl; stir to blend. Rub pork with chili powder mixture. Place pork in **CROCK-POT**® slow cooker.

2. Combine tomato sauce, 4 tablespoons honey, remaining 2 teaspoons chili powder, ½ teaspoon chipotle chili powder, ½ teaspoon cumin and ½ teaspoon garlic powder in large bowl. Pour tomato mixture over pork in **CROCK-POT**® slow cooker. Cover; cook on LOW 8 hours.

3. Remove pork to large bowl; cover with foil. Turn **CROCK-POT**® slow cooker to HIGH. Cook, partially covered, on HIGH 30 minutes or until thickened. Stir in remaining 1 tablespoon honey.

4. Remove bone from pork; discard. Shred pork using two forks. Stir shredded pork into **CROCK-POT**® slow cooker to coat with sauce. Serve with chips and coleslaw, if desired.

MAKES 8 SERVINGS

Shredded Chicken Tacos

2 pounds boneless, skinless chicken thighs

1 cup prepared mango salsa, plus additional for serving

8 (6-inch) yellow corn tortillas, warmed

Optional toppings: shredded pepper jack cheese, sour cream and/or lettuce

1. Coat inside of **CROCK-POT**® slow cooker with nonstick cooking spray. Add chicken and ½ cup salsa. Cover; cook on LOW 4 to 5 hours or on HIGH 2½ to 3 hours.

2. Remove chicken to large cutting board. Shred with two forks. Stir shredded chicken and remaining ½ cup salsa into **CROCK-POT**® slow cooker. Top as desired. Serve with additional salsa.

MAKES 4 SERVINGS

Crock and Go Ham with Pineapple Glaze

3 to 5 pounds ham

10 to 12 whole cloves

1 can (8 ounces) sliced pineapple, juice reserved and divided

2 tablespoons packed brown sugar

1 jar (4 ounces) maraschino cherries plus 1 tablespoon juice, reserved and divided

1. Stud ham with cloves. Place ham in **CROCK-POT**® slow cooker.

2. Combine reserved pineapple juice, brown sugar and reserved 1 tablespoon cherry juice in medium bowl; stir until glaze forms. Pour glaze over ham in **CROCK-POT**® slow cooker. Arrange sliced pineapple and cherries over ham. Cover; cook on LOW 6 to 8 hours. Remove cloves before serving.

MAKES 6 TO 8 SERVINGS

Shredded Chicken Tacos

Pot Roast with Bacon and Mushrooms

6 slices bacon

2½ to 3 pounds boneless beef chuck roast, trimmed

¾ teaspoon salt, divided

¼ teaspoon black pepper

¾ cup chopped shallots

8 ounces sliced white mushrooms

¼ ounce dried porcini mushrooms (optional)

4 cloves garlic, minced

1 teaspoon dried oregano

1 cup chicken broth

2 tablespoons tomato paste

Roasted Cauliflower (recipe follows, optional)

1. Heat large skillet over medium heat. Add bacon; cook 7 to 8 minutes until crisp. Remove to large paper towel-lined plate; crumble when cool enough to handle.

2. Pour off all but 2 tablespoons fat from skillet. Season roast with ½ teaspoon salt and pepper. Heat skillet over medium-high heat. Add roast; cook 8 minutes or until well browned. Remove to large plate. Add shallots, white mushrooms, porcini mushrooms, if desired, garlic, oregano and remaining ¼ teaspoon salt; cook 3 to 4 minutes or until softened. Remove shallot mixture to **CROCK-POT®** slow cooker.

3. Stir bacon into **CROCK-POT®** slow cooker. Place roast on top of vegetables. Combine broth and tomato paste in small bowl; stir to blend. Pour broth mixture over roast.

4. Cover; cook on LOW 8 hours. Remove roast to large cutting board. Let stand 10 minutes before slicing. Top with vegetables and cooking liquid. Serve with Roasted Cauliflower, if desired.

MAKES 6 TO 8 SERVINGS

ROASTED CAULIFLOWER: Preheat oven to 375°F. Break 1 head cauliflower into florets; place in large bowl. Drizzle with olive oil; toss to coat. Spread on baking sheet. Roast 20 minutes. Turn; roast 15 minutes. Makes 6 servings.

Shrimp Jambalaya

1 (8-ounce) box New Orleans style jambalaya mix

2½ cups water

1 can (about 14 ounces) diced tomatoes with green pepper, celery and onion

8 ounces andouille sausage, cut into ¼-inch-thick slices

1 teaspoon hot pepper sauce, plus additional for serving

1½ pounds large shrimp, peeled and deveined (with tails on)

1. Coat inside of **CROCK-POT**® slow cooker with nonstick cooking spray. Add jambalaya mix, water, tomatoes, sausage and 1 teaspoon hot pepper sauce; stir to blend. Cover; cook on LOW 2½ to 3 hours until rice is cooked through.

2. Stir in shrimp. Cover; cook on LOW 30 minutes or until shrimp are cooked through. Serve with additional hot pepper sauce.

MAKES 8 SERVINGS

Beef and Quinoa
Stuffed Cabbage Rolls

8 large green cabbage leaves, veins
   trimmed at bottom of each leaf

1 pound ground beef

1½ cups cooked quinoa

1 medium onion, chopped

1 cup tomato juice, divided

   Salt and black pepper

1. Heat salted water in large saucepan over high heat; bring to a boil. Add cabbage leaves; return to boil. Cook 2 minutes. Drain and let cool.

2. Combine beef, quinoa, onion and ¼ cup tomato juice in large bowl. Season with salt and pepper; mix well. Place cabbage leaf on large work surface; top center with 2 to 3 tablespoons beef mixture. Starting at stem end, roll up jelly-roll style, folding sides in as you go. Repeat with remaining cabbage rolls and beef mixture.

3. Place cabbage rolls seam side down and side by side in single layer in **CROCK-POT®** slow cooker. Pour in remaining ¾ cup tomato juice. Cover; cook on LOW 5 to 6 hours.

MAKES 4 SERVINGS

Sausage and Peppers over Polenta

1 to 1½ pounds Italian sausage

2 red and/or green bell peppers, sliced

1 medium onion, sliced

1 can (about 14 ounces) diced tomatoes with basil, oregano and garlic

1 tube (18 ounces) prepared polenta, cut into ½-inch-thick slices

Salt (optional)

1. Heat large skillet over medium heat. Add sausage; cook 8 minutes or until browned. Cut sausage into 1-inch pieces; place in **CROCK-POT**® slow cooker. Stir in bell peppers, onion and tomatoes. Cover; cook on LOW 5½ to 6 hours or until vegetables are tender.

2. Preheat broiler. Spray large baking sheet with nonstick cooking spray.

3. Place polenta on prepared baking sheet. Broil 2 to 3 minutes on each side or until heated through and lightly browned. Serve polenta topped with sausage mixture. Season with salt, if desired.

MAKES 4 SERVINGS

Braised Short Ribs with Aromatic Spices

3 pounds bone-in beef short ribs, trimmed

1 teaspoon ground cumin, divided

Salt

Black pepper

1 tablespoon olive oil

2 medium onions, halved and thinly sliced

10 cloves garlic, thinly sliced

2 tablespoons balsamic vinegar

2 tablespoons honey

1 cinnamon stick

2 star anise pods

2 large sweet potatoes, peeled and cut into ¾-inch cubes

1 cup beef broth

1. Season ribs with ½ teaspoon cumin, salt and pepper. Heat oil in large skillet over medium-high heat. Cook ribs 8 minutes or until browned, turning occasionally. Remove ribs to large plate.

2. Heat same skillet over medium heat. Add onions and garlic; cook 12 to 14 minutes or until onions are lightly browned. Stir in vinegar; cook 1 minute. Add remaining ½ teaspoon cumin, honey, cinnamon stick and star anise; cook and stir 30 seconds. Remove mixture to **CROCK-POT**® slow cooker. Stir in sweet potatoes; top with ribs. Pour in broth.

3. Cover; cook on LOW 8 to 9 hours or until meat is falling off the bones. Turn off heat. Remove and discard bones from ribs. Remove and discard cinnamon stick and star anise. Let cooking liquid stand 5 to 10 minutes. Skim off and discard fat. Serve meat with cooking liquid and vegetables.

MAKES 4 SERVINGS

Turkey Sausage and Quinoa Stuffed Peppers

4 medium red, yellow or orange bell peppers

½ cup uncooked quinoa, rinsed

1 cup water

12 ounces sweet Italian turkey sausage, casings removed and coarsely chopped

½ cup finely chopped zucchini

¼ cup chopped fresh basil

3 tablespoons tomato paste

½ teaspoon salt

¼ teaspoon black pepper

1¼ cups vegetable juice

Fresh basil leaves (optional)

1. Cut top ¼-inch off of each bell pepper. Remove and discard seeds.

2. Place quinoa in fine-mesh strainer; rinse well under cold running water. Bring water to a boil in small saucepan; stir in quinoa. Reduce heat to low; cover and simmer 10 to 15 minutes or until quinoa is tender and water is absorbed. Remove to large bowl; cool 5 minutes. Add sausage, zucchini, chopped basil, tomato paste, salt and black pepper to quinoa; mix well. Fill each bell pepper evenly with quinoa mixture.

3. Stand bell peppers in **CROCK-POT**® slow cooker. Pour ¼ cup vegetable juice over bell peppers; pour remaining 1 cup into bottom. Cover; cook on LOW 4 to 5 hours or on HIGH 2½ to 3 hours until filling is cooked through and bell peppers are tender. Serve bell peppers with cooking liquid. Garnish with basil leaves.

MAKES 4 SERVINGS

Pineapple and Pork Teriyaki

Nonstick cooking spray

2 pork tenderloins (1¼ pounds each)

1 can (8 ounces) pineapple chunks

½ cup teriyaki sauce

3 tablespoons honey

1 tablespoon minced fresh ginger

Hot cooked couscous or rice (optional)

1. Spray large skillet with nonstick cooking spray; heat over medium-high heat. Add pork; cook 8 minutes or until browned on all sides. Remove to oval-shaped **CROCK-POT**® slow cooker.

2. Combine pineapple, teriyaki sauce, honey and ginger in large bowl; stir to blend. Pour over pork. Cover; cook on LOW 6 to 7 hours or on HIGH 3 to 4 hours. Turn off heat. Remove pork to large cutting board. Let stand 15 minutes before slicing.

3. Let cooking liquid stand 5 to 10 minutes. Skim off and discard fat. Turn **CROCK-POT**® slow cooker to HIGH. Cook, partially covered, on HIGH 10 to 15 minutes or until sauce is thickened. Serve sliced pork with pineapple, cooking liquid and couscous, if desired.

MAKES 6 TO 8 SERVINGS

Coconut-Curry Chicken Thighs

8 chicken thighs (about 2 to 2½ pounds)

½ teaspoon salt

¼ teaspoon black pepper

1 tablespoon olive oil

1 medium onion, chopped

1 medium red bell pepper, chopped

3 cloves garlic, minced

1 tablespoon grated fresh ginger

1 can (about 13 ounces) coconut milk

3 tablespoons honey

1 tablespoon Thai red curry paste

2 teaspoons Thai roasted red chili paste

2 tablespoons chopped fresh cilantro (optional)

½ cup chopped cashew nuts (optional)

1. Coat inside of **CROCK-POT**® slow cooker with nonstick cooking spray. Season chicken with salt and black pepper. Heat oil in large skillet over medium-high heat. Add chicken; cook 6 to 8 minutes until browned. Remove to **CROCK-POT**® slow cooker.

2. Pour off all but 1 tablespoon of fat from skillet. Heat skillet over medium-high heat. Add onion, bell pepper, garlic and ginger; cook and stir 3 to 5 minutes or until vegetables begin to soften. Remove skillet from heat. Stir in coconut milk, honey, curry paste and chili paste until smooth. Pour coconut mixture over chicken in **CROCK-POT**® slow cooker.

3. Cover; cook on LOW 4 hours. Serve chicken with sauce. Garnish each serving with cilantro and cashews.

MAKES 4 SERVINGS

Pineapple and Butternut Squash Braised Chicken

- cut up chicken
- stir around

1 medium butternut squash, cut into 1-inch pieces (about 3 cups)

1 can (20 ounces) pineapple chunks

½ cup ketchup

2 tablespoons packed brown sugar

8 chicken thighs (about 2 pounds)

½ teaspoon salt

¼ teaspoon black pepper

1. Coat inside of **CROCK-POT**® slow cooker with nonstick cooking spray. Combine squash, pineapple with juice, ketchup and brown sugar in **CROCK-POT**® slow cooker. Season chicken with salt and pepper. Place chicken on top of squash mixture.

2. Cover; cook on LOW 5 to 6 hours. Remove chicken to large platter; cover with foil. Turn **CROCK-POT**® slow cooker to HIGH. Cook, uncovered, on HIGH 10 to 15 minutes or until sauce is thickened. Serve sauce over chicken.

MAKES 4 SERVINGS

Tomato and Red Wine Brisket

3 to 3½ pounds beef brisket, trimmed

¾ teaspoon salt, divided

¼ teaspoon black pepper

1 tablespoon olive oil

1 large red onion, sliced

½ cup dry red wine

1 can (28 ounces) diced tomatoes with basil, oregano and garlic

1. Coat inside of **CROCK-POT**® slow cooker with nonstick cooking spray. Season beef with ½ teaspoon salt and pepper. Heat oil in large skillet over medium-high heat. Add beef; cook 5 minutes or until browned on all sides. Remove to **CROCK-POT**® slow cooker.

2. Heat same skillet over medium-high heat. Add onion; cook and stir 5 minutes or until softened. Pour in wine. Bring mixture to a boil, scraping up any browned bits from bottom of skillet. Cook 3 to 4 minutes until wine is almost evaporated. Stir in tomatoes. Bring to a boil; cook 6 to 7 minutes or until slightly thickened. Stir in remaining ¼ teaspoon salt. Pour mixture over beef in **CROCK-POT**® slow cooker.

3. Cover; cook on LOW 7 to 8 hours. Remove beef to large cutting board; let stand 15 minutes before slicing. Turn **CROCK-POT**® slow cooker to HIGH. Cook, partially covered, on HIGH 10 minutes or until sauce is thickened. Serve sauce over brisket.

MAKES 8 SERVINGS

Braised Lamb Shanks

4 (12- to 16-ounce) lamb shanks
¾ teaspoon salt, divided
¼ teaspoon black pepper
1 tablespoon olive oil
1 medium onion, chopped
2 stalks celery, chopped
2 carrots, chopped

6 cloves garlic, minced
1 teaspoon dried basil
1 can (about 14 ounces) diced tomatoes
2 tablespoons tomato paste
Fresh Italian parsley (optional)

1. Coat inside of **CROCK-POT**® slow cooker with nonstick cooking spray. Season lamb with ½ teaspoon salt and pepper. Heat oil in large skillet over medium-high heat. Add lamb; cook 8 to 10 minutes or until browned on all sides. Remove lamb to **CROCK-POT**® slow cooker.

2. Return same skillet to medium-high heat. Add onion, celery, carrots, garlic and basil; cook and stir 3 to 4 minutes or until vegetables are softened. Add tomatoes, tomato paste and remaining ¼ teaspoon salt; cook and stir 2 to 3 minutes or until slightly thickened. Pour tomato mixture over lamb shanks in **CROCK-POT**® slow cooker.

3. Cover; cook on LOW 8 to 9 hours or until lamb is very tender. Remove lamb to large serving plate. Cover loosely with foil. Turn **CROCK-POT**® slow cooker to HIGH. Cook, uncovered, on HIGH 10 to 15 minutes or until sauce is thickened. Serve lamb with sauce. Garnish with parsley.

MAKES 4 SERVINGS

Tofu Tikka Masala

1 package (14 to 16 ounces) extra firm tofu, cut into 1-inch pieces

½ cup whole milk yogurt

2 teaspoons salt, divided

1 tablespoon plus 1 teaspoon minced garlic, divided

2½ teaspoons grated fresh ginger, divided

2 tablespoons vegetable oil

1 medium onion, chopped

2 tablespoons tomato paste

1 tablespoon garam masala

1 can (28 ounces) crushed tomatoes

1 teaspoon sugar

½ cup whipping cream

3 tablespoons chopped fresh cilantro

Hot cooked basmati rice

1. Combine tofu, yogurt, 1 teaspoon salt, 1 teaspoon garlic and 1 teaspoon ginger in large bowl; stir to blend. Cover; refrigerate 1 hour or overnight.

2. Heat oil in large skillet over medium heat. Add onion; cook and stir 8 minutes or until softened. Add remaining 1 tablespoon garlic, remaining 1½ teaspoons ginger, remaining 1 teaspoon salt, tomato paste and garam masala; cook and stir 1 minute. Add tomatoes and sugar; bring to a simmer. Place in **CROCK-POT**® slow cooker. Place tofu in **CROCK-POT**® slow cooker using slotted spoon; discard yogurt mixture. Stir gently.

3. Cover; cook on LOW 8 hours. Stir in whipping cream and cilantro. Serve over rice.

MAKES 4 TO 6 SERVINGS

Mexican Carnitas

2 pounds boneless pork shoulder roast
1 tablespoon garlic salt
1 tablespoon black pepper
1½ teaspoons adobo seasoning
1 medium onion, chopped
1 jar (16 ounces) green salsa
½ cup water

¼ cup chopped fresh cilantro
Juice of 2 medium limes
3 cloves garlic, minced
4 (6-inch) flour tortillas, warmed
Optional toppings: chopped green bell pepper, tomatoes and red onion
Lime wedges (optional)

1. Coat inside of **CROCK-POT®** slow cooker with nonstick cooking spray. Season pork with garlic salt, black pepper and adobo seasoning.

2. Place pork, onion, salsa, water, cilantro, lime juice and garlic in **CROCK-POT®** slow cooker. Cover; cook on LOW 4 to 5 hours. Serve in tortillas with desired toppings and lime wedges.

MAKES 2 SERVINGS

Southern Smothered Pork Chops

8 pounds pork chops
  Salt and black pepper
2 tablespoons vegetable oil
3 cups water
1 can (10½ ounces) cream of
  mushroom soup
1 large onion, chopped

5 cloves garlic, chopped
2 tablespoons Italian seasoning
1 package (about ½ ounce) pork
  gravy mix
1 package (about 1 ounce) dry
  mushroom and onion soup mix
  Corn on the cob (optional)

1. Season pork with salt and pepper. Heat oil in large skillet over medium-high heat. Add pork; brown 3 to 4 minutes on each side.

2. Place pork, water, soup, onion, garlic, Italian seasoning, gravy mix and soup mix in **CROCK-POT**® slow cooker. Cover; cook on LOW 5 hours. Serve with corn, if desired.

MAKES 6 TO 8 SERVINGS

Summer Squash Lasagna

3 tablespoons olive oil, divided

1 large onion, chopped

¾ teaspoon salt, divided

2 cloves garlic, minced

2 medium zucchini (about 1 pound), cut lengthwise into ¼-inch strips

2 yellow squash (about 1 pound), cut lengthwise into ¼-inch strips

1 container (15 ounces) ricotta cheese

1 egg

¼ cup plus 2 tablespoons chopped fresh basil, divided

¼ teaspoon black pepper

½ cup shredded or freshly grated Parmesan cheese, divided

1 jar (about 26 ounces) marinara sauce

12 uncooked curly lasagna noodles

1 package (8 ounces) shredded mozzarella cheese, divided

1. Coat inside of **CROCK-POT**® slow cooker with nonstick cooking spray. Heat 1 tablespoon oil in large skillet over medium-high heat. Add onion and ¼ teaspoon salt; cook and stir 5 minutes or until softened. Add garlic; cook and stir 1 minute. Remove to large bowl.

2. Heat 1 tablespoon oil in same skillet. Add half of zucchini, half of squash and ¼ teaspoon salt; cook and stir 5 minutes or until lightly browned. Remove mixture to bowl with onion. Repeat with remaining 1 tablespoon oil, squash and ¼ teaspoon salt.

3. Combine ricotta cheese, egg, ¼ cup basil, pepper and ¼ cup Parmesan cheese in medium bowl; stir to blend.

4. Pour ½ cup marinara sauce evenly into bottom of **CROCK-POT**® slow cooker. Top with 3 lasagna noodles, breaking to fit evenly; layer with ⅔ cup ricotta mixture, ⅓ squash mixture, ¼ cup mozzarella and ½ cup marinara sauce. Repeat layers twice. Top with remaining 3 lasagna noodles, marinara sauce and mozzarella. Sprinkle with remaining ¼ cup Parmesan cheese.

5. Cover; cook on LOW 3 hours. Turn off heat. Uncover; let stand 30 minutes. Sprinkle with remaining 2 tablespoons basil before cutting and serving.

MAKES 6 TO 8 SERVINGS

Coq au Vin with Lima Beans

4 pounds chicken thighs and drumsticks

3 slices bacon, cut into pieces

4 cups chicken broth

1 cup sliced mushrooms

1 cup sliced carrots

1 cup dry red wine

½ cup pearl onions

⅓ cup whiskey

3 to 4 cloves garlic, chopped

2 tablespoons tomato paste

1½ teaspoons herbes de Provence

2 whole bay leaves

Salt and black pepper

1 tablespoon water

2 tablespoons all-purpose flour

1 cup lima beans

Chopped fresh Italian parsley (optional)

Roasted red potatoes, quartered (optional)

1. Coat inside of **CROCK-POT®** slow cooker with nonstick cooking spray. Add chicken and bacon. Cover; cook on HIGH 45 minutes.

2. Turn **CROCK-POT®** slow cooker to LOW. Add broth, mushrooms, carrots, wine, onions, whiskey, garlic, tomato paste, herbes de Provence and bay leaves. Stir water into flour in small bowl until smooth. Whisk into **CROCK-POT®** slow cooker. Cover; cook on LOW 6 hours. Add beans to **CROCK-POT®** slow cooker during last 10 minutes of cooking. Remove and discard bay leaves. Garnish with parsley. Serve with potatoes, if desired.

MAKES 8 TO 10 SERVINGS

Satisfying
Side Dishes

Deluxe Potato Casserole

1   can (10¾ ounces) condensed
    cream of chicken soup, undiluted
1   container (8 ounces) sour cream
¼   cup chopped onion
¼   cup (½ stick) plus 3 tablespoons
    melted butter, divided

1   teaspoon salt
2   pounds red potatoes, peeled
    and diced
2   cups (8 ounces) shredded
    Cheddar cheese
1½ to 2 cups stuffing mix

1. Combine soup, sour cream, onion, ¼ cup butter and salt in small bowl.

2. Combine potatoes and cheese in **CROCK-POT**® slow cooker. Pour soup mixture over potato mixture; mix well. Sprinkle stuffing mix over potato mixture; drizzle with remaining 3 tablespoons butter. Cover; cook on LOW 8 to 10 hours or on HIGH 5 to 6 hours.

MAKES 8 TO 10 SERVINGS

Thai Red Curry with Tofu

1 medium sweet potato, peeled and cut into 1-inch pieces

1 small eggplant, halved lengthwise and cut crosswise into ½-inch slices

8 ounces extra firm tofu, cut into 1-inch cubes

½ cup green beans, cut into 1-inch pieces

½ red bell pepper, cut into ¼-inch-wide strips

2 tablespoons vegetable oil

5 medium shallots (about 1½ cups), thinly sliced

3 tablespoons Thai red curry paste

1 teaspoon minced garlic

1 teaspoon grated fresh ginger

1 can (about 13 ounces) coconut milk

1½ tablespoons soy sauce

1 tablespoon packed light brown sugar

¼ cup chopped fresh basil

2 tablespoons lime juice

Hot cooked rice (optional)

1. Coat inside of **CROCK-POT**® slow cooker with nonstick cooking spray. Add sweet potato, eggplant, tofu, green beans and bell pepper.

2. Heat oil in large skillet over medium heat. Add shallots; cook and stir 5 minutes or until browned and tender. Add curry paste, garlic and ginger; cook and stir 1 minute. Add coconut milk, soy sauce and brown sugar; bring to a simmer. Pour mixture over vegetables in **CROCK-POT**® slow cooker.

3. Cover; cook on LOW 2 to 3 hours. Stir in basil and lime juice. Serve over rice, if desired.

MAKES 4 SERVINGS

Five-Ingredient Mushroom Stuffing

6 tablespoons butter

2 medium onions, chopped

1 pound sliced white mushrooms

¼ teaspoon salt

5 cups bagged stuffing mix, any seasoning

1 cup vegetable broth

Chopped fresh Italian parsley

1. Melt butter in large skillet over medium heat. Add onions, mushrooms and salt; cook and stir 20 minutes or until vegetables are browned and most of liquid is evaporated. Remove onion mixture to **CROCK-POT**® slow cooker.

2. Stir in stuffing mix and broth. Cover; cook on LOW 3 hours. Garnish with parsley.

MAKES 12 SERVINGS

Lemon and Tangerine Glazed Carrots

6 cups sliced carrots

1½ cups apple juice

6 tablespoons butter

¼ cup packed brown sugar

2 tablespoons grated lemon peel

2 tablespoons grated tangerine peel

½ teaspoon salt

Chopped fresh Italian parsley (optional)

Combine carrots, apple juice, butter, brown sugar, lemon peel, tangerine peel and salt in **CROCK-POT**® slow cooker; stir to blend. Cover; cook on LOW 4 to 5 hours or on HIGH 1 to 3 hours. Garnish with parsley.

MAKES 10 TO 12 SERVINGS

Five-Ingredient Mushroom Stuffing

Creamy Curried Spinach

3 packages (10 ounces *each*) frozen
   spinach

1 onion, chopped

4 teaspoons minced garlic

2 tablespoons curry powder

2 tablespoons butter, melted

¼ cup chicken broth

¼ cup whipping cream

1 teaspoon lemon juice

Combine spinach, onion, garlic, curry powder, butter and broth in **CROCK-POT®**
slow cooker; stir to blend. Cover; cook on LOW 3 to 4 hours or on HIGH 2 hours. Stir
in whipping cream and lemon juice during last 30 minutes of cooking.

MAKES 6 TO 8 SERVINGS

Olive Oil Mashed Rutabagas

1 (2½- to 3-pound) rutabaga
    (waxed turnip), peeled and
    cut into 1-inch pieces
4 cloves garlic

Boiling water
2 tablespoons olive oil
1 teaspoon salt
1 teaspoon dried thyme

1. Combine rutabaga, garlic and enough boiling water to cover by 1 inch in **CROCK-POT®** slow cooker. Cover; cook on LOW 7 to 8 hours.

2. Place rutabaga in food processor or blender; purée, adding water as necessary to reach desired consistency. Stir in oil, salt and thyme.

MAKES 8 SERVINGS

Gratin Potatoes with Asiago Cheese

6 slices bacon, cut into 1-inch pieces
6 medium baking potatoes, thinly
    sliced

½ cup grated Asiago cheese
    Salt and black pepper
1½ cups whipping cream

1. Heat large skillet over medium heat. Add bacon; cook and stir until crisp. Remove to paper towel-lined plate using slotted spoon.

2. Pour bacon drippings into **CROCK-POT®** slow cooker. Layer one fourth of potatoes on bottom of **CROCK-POT®** slow cooker. Sprinkle one fourth of bacon over potatoes; top with one fourth of cheese. Season with salt and pepper.

3. Repeat layers three times. Pour whipping cream over all. Cover; cook on LOW 7 to 9 hours or on HIGH 5 to 6 hours.

MAKES 4 TO 6 SERVINGS

Olive Oil Mashed Rutabagas

BBQ Baked Beans

3 cans (about 15 ounces *each*) white beans, drained

4 slices bacon, chopped

¾ cup prepared barbecue sauce

½ cup maple syrup

1½ teaspoons ground mustard

Coat inside of **CROCK-POT**® slow cooker with nonstick cooking spray. Add beans, bacon, barbecue sauce, syrup and ground mustard; stir to blend. Cover; cook on LOW 4 hours, stirring halfway through cooking time.

MAKES 12 SERVINGS

Lentils with Walnuts

3 cups chicken broth

1 cup dried brown lentils, rinsed and sorted

1 small onion or shallot, chopped

1 stalk celery, trimmed and chopped

1 large carrot, chopped

¼ teaspoon dried thyme

Salt and black pepper

¼ cup chopped walnuts

1. Combine broth, lentils, onion, celery, carrot and thyme in **CROCK-POT**® slow cooker; stir to blend. Cover; cook on HIGH 3 hours or until most of broth is absorbed.

2. Season with salt and pepper. Spoon lentils into serving bowl and sprinkle with walnuts.

MAKES 4 TO 6 SERVINGS

SERVING SUGGESTION: Top dish with 4 bacon slices, crisp-cooked and crumbled, if desired.

Satisfying Side Dishes

BBQ Baked Beans

Farro Risotto
with Mushrooms and Spinach

2 tablespoons olive oil, divided

1 onion, chopped

12 ounces cremini mushrooms, stems trimmed, quartered

¾ teaspoon salt

¼ teaspoon black pepper

2 cloves garlic, minced

1 cup uncooked farro

1 sprig fresh thyme

4 cups vegetable broth

8 ounces baby spinach

½ cup shredded Parmesan cheese, plus additional for garnish

1. Heat 1 tablespoon oil in large skillet over medium heat. Add onion; cook and stir 8 minutes or until tender. Remove to **CROCK-POT**® slow cooker.

2. Add remaining 1 tablespoon oil to same skillet; heat over medium-high heat. Add mushrooms, salt and pepper; cook 6 to 8 minutes or until mushrooms have released their liquid and are browned. Add garlic; cook 1 minute. Stir in farro and thyme; cook 1 minute. Remove mushroom mixture to **CROCK-POT**® slow cooker. Stir in broth.

3. Cover; cook on HIGH 3½ hours until farro is tender and broth is absorbed. Remove thyme sprig. Stir in spinach and ½ cup cheese just before serving. Garnish with additional cheese.

MAKES 4 SERVINGS

Cheesy Polenta

6 cups vegetable broth

1½ cups uncooked medium-grind instant polenta

½ cup shredded or freshly grated Parmesan cheese, plus additional for serving

¼ cup (½ stick) butter, cut into pieces

Fried sage (see Note, optional)

1. Coat inside of **CROCK-POT®** slow cooker with nonstick cooking spray. Heat broth in large saucepan over high heat. Remove to **CROCK-POT®** slow cooker; whisk in polenta.

2. Cover; cook on LOW 2 to 2½ hours or until polenta is tender and creamy. Stir in cheese and ¼ cup butter. Serve with additional butter and garnish with fried sage.

MAKES 6 SERVINGS

TIP: Spread any leftover polenta in a baking dish and refrigerate until cold. Cut cold polenta into sticks or slices. Fry or grill the polenta until lightly browned and heated through.

NOTE: To fry sage leaves, melt 1 tablespoon butter in small skillet over medium heat. Add fresh sage leaves; cook until crisp and lightly browned.

Curried Cauliflower and Potatoes

3 tablespoons vegetable oil

1 medium onion, chopped

1 tablespoon minced garlic

1 tablespoon curry powder

1½ teaspoons salt, plus additional for seasoning

1½ teaspoons grated fresh ginger

1 teaspoon ground turmeric

1 teaspoon yellow or brown mustard seeds

¼ teaspoon red pepper flakes

1 medium head cauliflower, cut into 1-inch pieces

2 pounds fingerling potatoes, cut in half

½ cup water

1. Heat oil in medium skillet over medium heat. Add onion; cook and stir 8 minutes or until softened. Add garlic, curry powder, 1½ teaspoons salt, ginger, turmeric, mustard seeds and red pepper flakes; cook and stir 1 minute. Remove to **CROCK-POT**® slow cooker.

2. Stir in cauliflower, potatoes and water. Cover; cook on HIGH 4 hours. Season with additional salt, if desired.

MAKES 4 TO 6 SERVINGS

Mushroom Wild Rice

1½ cups chicken broth
1 cup uncooked wild rice
½ cup diced onion
½ cup sliced mushrooms

½ cup diced red or green
    bell pepper
1 tablespoon olive oil
Salt and black pepper

Combine broth, rice, onion, mushrooms, bell pepper and oil in **CROCK-POT**®
slow cooker; stir to blend. Season with salt and black pepper. Cover; cook on
HIGH 2½ hours or until rice is tender and liquid is absorbed.

MAKES 8 SERVINGS

Cheesy Corn and Peppers

2 pounds frozen corn
2 poblano peppers, chopped
2 tablespoons butter, cut into pieces
1 teaspoon salt
½ teaspoon ground cumin

¼ teaspoon black pepper
3 ounces cream cheese, cut into
    pieces
1 cup (4 ounces) shredded sharp
    Cheddar cheese

1. Coat inside of **CROCK-POT**® slow cooker with nonstick cooking spray. Combine
corn, poblano peppers, butter, salt, cumin and black pepper in **CROCK-POT**® slow
cooker. Cover; cook on HIGH 2 hours.

2. Stir in cheeses. Cover; cook on HIGH 15 minutes or until cheeses are melted.

MAKES 8 SERVINGS

Mushroom Wild Rice

Candied Sweet Potatoes

3 medium sweet potatoes (1½ to 2 pounds), peeled and sliced into ½-inch rounds

½ cup water

¼ cup (½ stick) butter, cut into pieces

2 tablespoons sugar

1 tablespoon vanilla

1 teaspoon ground nutmeg

Combine sweet potatoes, water, butter, sugar, vanilla and nutmeg in **CROCK-POT®** slow cooker; stir to blend. Cover; cook on LOW 7 hours or on HIGH 4 hours.

MAKES 4 SERVINGS

Collard Greens

1 tablespoon olive oil

3 turkey necks

5 bunches collard greens, stemmed and chopped

5 cups vegetable broth

1 small onion, chopped

2 cloves garlic, minced

1 tablespoon apple cider vinegar

1 teaspoon sugar

Salt and black pepper

Red pepper flakes (optional)

1. Heat oil in large skillet over medium-high heat. Add turkey necks; cook and stir 3 to 5 minutes or until brown.

2. Combine turkey necks, collard greens, broth, onion and garlic in **CROCK-POT®** slow cooker; stir to blend. Cover; cook on LOW 5 to 6 hours. Remove and discard turkey necks. Stir in vinegar, sugar, salt, black pepper and red pepper flakes, if desired.

MAKES 12 SERVINGS

Candied Sweet Potatoes

Quinoa and Vegetable Medley

2 medium sweet potatoes, peeled and cut into ½-inch-thick slices

1 medium eggplant, cut into ½-inch cubes

1 large green bell pepper, sliced

1 medium tomato, cut into wedges

1 small onion, cut into wedges

½ teaspoon salt

¼ teaspoon ground red pepper

¼ teaspoon black pepper

1 cup uncooked quinoa

2 cups vegetable broth

2 cloves garlic, minced

½ teaspoon dried thyme

¼ teaspoon dried marjoram

1. Coat inside of **CROCK-POT**® slow cooker with nonstick cooking spray. Combine sweet potatoes, eggplant, bell pepper, tomato, onion, salt, ground red pepper and black pepper in **CROCK-POT**® slow cooker; toss to coat.

2. Place quinoa in strainer; rinse well. Add quinoa to vegetable mixture in **CROCK-POT**® slow cooker. Stir in broth, garlic, thyme and marjoram. Cover; cook on LOW 5 hours or on HIGH 2½ hours or until broth is absorbed.

MAKES 6 SERVINGS

French Carrot Medley

2 cups sliced carrots

¾ cup orange juice

1 can (4 ounces) sliced mushrooms, undrained

4 stalks celery, sliced

2 tablespoons chopped onion

½ teaspoon dried dill weed

Salt and black pepper

¼ cup cold water

2 teaspoons cornstarch

Sprigs fresh dill (optional)

1. Combine carrots, orange juice, mushrooms, celery, onion and dried dill weed in **CROCK-POT®** slow cooker. Season with salt and pepper. Cover; cook on LOW 3 to 4 hours or on HIGH 2 hours.

2. Stir water into cornstarch in small bowl until smooth; whisk into cooking liquid. Cover; cook on HIGH 15 minutes or until sauce is thickened. Spoon sauce over vegetable mixture before serving. Garnish with fresh dill.

MAKES 6 SERVINGS

Chunky Ranch Potatoes

3 pounds unpeeled red potatoes, quartered

1 cup water

½ cup prepared ranch dressing

½ cup grated Parmesan cheese

¼ cup minced fresh chives

1. Place potatoes in **CROCK-POT®** slow cooker. Add water. Cover; cook on LOW 7 to 9 hours or on HIGH 4 to 6 hours.

2. Stir in ranch dressing, cheese and chives. Break up potatoes into large pieces.

MAKES 8 SERVINGS

Mashed Root Vegetables

1 pound potatoes, peeled and cut into 1-inch pieces

1 pound turnips, peeled and cut into 1-inch pieces

12 ounces sweet potatoes, peeled and cut into 1-inch pieces

8 ounces parsnips, peeled and cut into ½-inch pieces

5 tablespoons butter

¼ cup water

2 teaspoons salt

¼ teaspoon black pepper

1 cup milk

1. Coat inside of **CROCK-POT®** slow cooker with nonstick cooking spray. Add potatoes, turnips, sweet potatoes, parsnips, butter, water, salt and pepper; stir to blend. Cover; cook on HIGH 3 to 4 hours.

2. Mash mixture with potato masher until smooth. Stir in milk. Cover; cook on HIGH 15 minutes.

MAKES 6 SERVINGS

Chunky Ranch Potatoes

Fennel Braised with Tomato

2 fennel bulbs
1 tablespoon olive oil
1 onion, sliced
1 clove garlic, sliced
4 tomatoes, chopped

⅔ cup vegetable broth
3 tablespoons dry white wine
1 tablespoon chopped fresh marjoram *or* 1 teaspoon dried marjoram
Salt and black pepper

1. Trim stems and bottoms from fennel bulbs, reserving green leafy tops for garnish. Cut each bulb lengthwise into four wedges.

2. Heat oil in large skillet over medium heat. Add fennel, onion and garlic; cook and stir 5 minutes or until onion is soft and translucent. Remove fennel mixture to **CROCK-POT**® slow cooker. Add tomatoes, broth, wine, marjoram, salt and pepper; stir to blend.

3. Cover; cook on LOW 2 to 3 hours or on HIGH 1 to 1½ hours. Garnish with reserved green leafy fennel tops.

MAKES 6 SERVINGS

Slow-Cooked Succotash

2 teaspoons olive oil
1 cup diced onion
1 cup diced green bell pepper
1 cup diced celery
1 teaspoon paprika
1½ cups frozen corn

1½ cups frozen lima beans
1 cup canned diced tomatoes
2 teaspoons dried parsley flakes *or* 1 tablespoon minced fresh Italian parsley
Salt and black pepper

1. Heat oil in large skillet over medium heat. Add onion, bell pepper and celery; cook and stir 5 minutes or until vegetables are crisp-tender. Stir in paprika.

2. Stir onion mixture, corn, beans, tomatoes and parsley flakes into **CROCK-POT**® slow cooker. Season with salt and black pepper. Cover; cook on LOW 6 to 8 hours or on HIGH 3 to 4 hours.

MAKES 8 SERVINGS

Blue Cheese Potatoes

2 pounds red potatoes, peeled and cut into ½-inch pieces
1¼ cups chopped green onions, divided
2 tablespoons olive oil, divided

1 teaspoon dried basil
½ teaspoon salt
¼ teaspoon black pepper
½ cup crumbled blue cheese

1. Layer potatoes, 1 cup green onions, 1 tablespoon oil, basil, salt and pepper in **CROCK-POT**® slow cooker. Cover; cook on LOW 7 hours or on HIGH 4 hours.

2. Gently stir in cheese and remaining 1 tablespoon oil. Cover; cook on HIGH 5 minutes. Remove potatoes to large serving platter; top with remaining ¼ cup green onions.

MAKES 5 SERVINGS

Slow-Cooked Succotash

Brussels Sprouts
with Bacon, Thyme and Raisins

2 pounds Brussels sprouts

1 cup chicken broth

⅔ cup golden raisins

2 thick slices applewood smoked bacon, chopped

2 tablespoons chopped fresh thyme

Trim ends from sprouts; cut in half lengthwise through core (or in quarters). Combine sprouts, broth, raisins, bacon and thyme in **CROCK-POT**® slow cooker; stir to blend. Cover; cook on LOW 3 to 4 hours.

MAKES 8 SERVINGS

Cheesy Mashed Potato Casserole

4 pounds Yukon Gold potatoes, cut into 1-inch pieces

2 cups vegetable broth

3 tablespoons unsalted butter, cubed

½ cup milk, heated

⅓ cup sour cream

2 cups (8 ounces) shredded sharp Cheddar cheese, plus additional for garnish

½ teaspoon salt

¼ teaspoon black pepper

1. Coat inside of **CROCK-POT**® slow cooker with nonstick cooking spray. Add potatoes and broth; dot with butter. Cover; cook on LOW 4½ to 5 hours.

2. Mash potatoes with potato masher; stir in milk, sour cream, 2 cups cheese, salt and pepper until cheese is melted. Garnish with additional cheese.

MAKES 10 TO 12 SERVINGS

Brussels Sprouts with Bacon, Thyme and Raisins

Roasted Summer Squash with Pine Nuts and Romano Cheese

2 tablespoons olive oil

½ cup chopped yellow onion

1 medium red bell pepper, chopped

1 clove garlic, minced

3 medium zucchini, cut into ½-inch slices

3 medium summer squash, cut into ½-inch slices

½ cup chopped pine nuts

⅓ cup grated Romano cheese

1 teaspoon Italian seasoning

1 teaspoon salt

¼ teaspoon black pepper

1 tablespoon unsalted butter, cubed

Sprigs fresh basil (optional)

1. Heat oil in large skillet over medium-high heat. Add onion, bell pepper and garlic; cook and stir 10 minutes or until onion is translucent and soft. Remove to **CROCK-POT®** slow cooker. Add zucchini and summer squash; toss lightly.

2. Combine pine nuts, cheese, Italian seasoning, salt and black pepper in small bowl. Fold half of cheese mixture into squash mixture. Sprinkle remaining cheese mixture on top. Dot with butter. Cover; cook on LOW 4 to 6 hours. Garnish with basil.

MAKES 6 TO 8 SERVINGS

Satisfying Side Dishes

Orange-Spice Glazed Carrots

1 package (32 ounces) baby carrots
½ cup packed light brown sugar
½ cup orange juice
3 tablespoons butter
¾ teaspoon ground cinnamon
¼ teaspoon ground nutmeg
¼ cup cold water
2 tablespoons cornstarch
Orange peel (optional)

1. Combine carrots, brown sugar, orange juice, butter, cinnamon and nutmeg in **CROCK-POT®** slow cooker; stir to blend. Cover; cook on LOW 3½ to 4 hours.

2. Spoon carrots into large serving bowl; cover loosely with foil. Turn **CROCK-POT®** slow cooker to HIGH.

3. Stir water into cornstarch in small bowl until smooth; whisk into cooking liquid. Cover; cook on HIGH 15 minutes or until thickened. Spoon over carrots. Garnish with orange peel.

MAKES 6 SERVINGS

Braised Beets with Cranberries

2½ pounds medium beets, peeled
    and cut into wedges

1   cup cranberry juice

½   cup sweetened dried cranberries

2   tablespoons quick-cooking
    tapioca

2   tablespoons butter, cut into pieces

2   tablespoons honey

½   teaspoon salt

⅓   cup crumbled blue cheese
    (optional)

    Orange peel (optional)

1. Combine beets, cranberry juice, cranberries, tapioca, butter, honey and salt in **CROCK-POT**® slow cooker; stir to blend. Cover; cook on LOW 7 to 8 hours.

2. Remove beets to large serving bowl using slotted spoon. Pour half of cooking liquid over beets. Garnish with blue cheese and orange peel.

MAKES 6 TO 8 SERVINGS

Braised Beets with Cranberries

Coconut-Lime Sweet Potatoes with Walnuts

2½ pounds sweet potatoes, peeled and cut into 1-inch pieces

8 ounces shredded carrots

¾ cup shredded coconut, toasted and divided*

¼ cup (½ stick) butter, melted

3 tablespoons sugar

½ teaspoon salt

¾ cup walnuts, toasted, coarsely chopped**

2 teaspoons grated lime peel

*To toast coconut, spread evenly on ungreased baking sheet. Toast in preheated 350°F oven 5 to 7 minutes or until light golden brown, stirring occasionally.

**To toast walnuts, spread in single layer in small heavy skillet. Cook and stir over medium heat 1 to 2 minutes or until lightly browned.

1. Combine potatoes, carrots, ½ cup coconut, butter, sugar and salt in **CROCK-POT®** slow cooker. Cover; cook on LOW 5 to 6 hours.

2. Remove to large bowl. Mash potatoes with potato masher. Stir in walnuts and lime peel. Sprinkle with remaining ¼ cup coconut.

MAKES 6 TO 8 SERVINGS

Cran-Orange Acorn Squash

5 tablespoons uncooked instant brown rice

3 tablespoons minced onion

3 tablespoons diced celery

3 tablespoons dried cranberries

Pinch ground sage

3 small acorn or carnival squash, cut in half

1 teaspoon butter, cubed

3 tablespoons orange juice

½ cup warm water

1. Combine rice, onion, celery, cranberries and sage in small bowl; stir to blend. Stuff each squash with rice mixture; dot with butter. Pour ½ tablespoon orange juice into each squash half over stuffing.

2. Stand squash in **CROCK-POT**® slow cooker. Pour water into **CROCK-POT**® slow cooker. Cover; cook on LOW 2½ hours or until squash is tender.

MAKES 6 SERVINGS

Parmesan Potato Wedges

2 pounds red potatoes, cut into ½-inch wedges

¼ cup finely chopped yellow onion

1½ teaspoons dried oregano

½ teaspoon salt

¼ teaspoon black pepper

2 tablespoons butter, cubed

¼ cup grated Parmesan cheese

Layer potatoes, onion, oregano, salt and pepper in **CROCK-POT**® slow cooker; dot with butter. Cover; cook on HIGH 4 hours. Remove potatoes to large serving platter; sprinkle with cheese.

MAKES 6 SERVINGS

Cran-Orange Acorn Squash

Cheesy Cauliflower

3 pounds cauliflower florets

¼ cup water

5 tablespoons unsalted butter

1 cup finely chopped onion

6 tablespoons all-purpose flour

¼ teaspoon dry mustard

2 cups milk

2 cups (8 ounces) shredded sharp Cheddar cheese

Salt and black pepper

1. Coat inside of **CROCK-POT**® slow cooker with nonstick cooking spray. Add cauliflower and water.

2. Melt butter in medium saucepan over medium-high heat. Add onion; cook 4 to 5 minutes or until slightly softened. Add flour and mustard; cook and stir 3 minutes or until well combined. Whisk in milk until smooth. Bring to a boil; cook 1 to 2 minutes or until thickened. Stir in cheese; season with salt and pepper. Cook and stir until cheese is melted. Pour cheese mixture over top of cauliflower in **CROCK-POT**® slow cooker. Cover; cook on LOW 4 to 4½ hours.

MAKES 8 TO 10 SERVINGS

Corn on the Cob with Garlic Herb Butter

4 to 5 ears of corn, husked

½ cup (1 stick) unsalted butter, softened

3 to 4 cloves garlic, minced

2 tablespoons finely minced fresh Italian parsley

Salt and black pepper

1. Place each ear of corn on a piece of foil. Combine butter, garlic and parsley in small bowl; spread onto corn. Season with salt and pepper; tightly seal foil.

2. Place in **CROCK-POT**® slow cooker, overlapping ears, if necessary. Add enough water to come one fourth of the way up sides of **CROCK-POT**® slow cooker. Cover; cook on LOW 4 to 5 hours or on HIGH 2 to 2½ hours.

MAKES 4 TO 5 SERVINGS

Asparagus and Cheese

1½ pounds fresh asparagus, trimmed

2 cups crushed saltine crackers

1 can (10¾ ounces) condensed cream of asparagus soup, undiluted

1 can (10¾ ounces) condensed cream of chicken or cream of celery soup, undiluted

4 ounces American cheese, cubed

⅔ cup slivered almonds

1 egg

Combine asparagus, crackers, soups, cheese, almonds and egg in **CROCK-POT**® slow cooker; toss to coat. Cover; cook on HIGH 3 to 3½ hours.

MAKES 4 TO 6 SERVINGS

Corn on the Cob with Garlic Herb Butter

Delicious Desserts

Peach Cobbler

- 2 packages (16 ounces *each*) frozen peaches, thawed and drained
- ½ cup plus 1 tablespoon sugar, divided
- 2 teaspoons ground cinnamon, divided
- ½ teaspoon ground nutmeg
- ¾ cup all-purpose flour
- 6 tablespoons butter, cut into pieces
- Whipped cream (optional)

1. Combine peaches, ½ cup sugar, 1½ teaspoons cinnamon and nutmeg in **CROCK-POT**® slow cooker; stir to blend.

2. Combine flour, remaining 1 tablespoon sugar and remaining ½ teaspoon cinnamon in small bowl. Cut in butter with pastry blender or two knives until mixture resembles coarse crumbs. Sprinkle over peach mixture.

3. Cover; cook on HIGH 2 hours. Serve with whipped cream, if desired.

MAKES 4 TO 6 SERVINGS

Spiced Vanilla Applesauce

5 pounds (about 10 medium) sweet apples (such as Fuji or Gala), peeled and cut into 1-inch pieces

½ cup water

2 teaspoons vanilla

1 teaspoon cinnamon

¼ teaspoon grated nutmeg

¼ teaspoon cloves

1. Combine apples, water, vanilla, cinnamon, nutmeg and cloves in **CROCK-POT®** slow cooker; stir to blend. Cover; cook on HIGH 3 to 4 hours until apples are very tender.

2. Turn off heat. Mash mixture with potato masher to smooth out any large lumps. Let cool completely before serving.

MAKES 6 CUPS

Cherry Flan

5 eggs

½ cup sugar

½ teaspoon salt

¾ cup all-purpose flour

1 can (12 ounces) evaporated milk

1 teaspoon vanilla

1 bag (16 ounces) frozen pitted dark sweet cherries, thawed

Whipped cream or cherry vanilla ice cream

1. Coat inside of **CROCK-POT®** slow cooker with nonstick cooking spray. Beat eggs, sugar and salt in large bowl with electric mixer at high speed until thick and pale yellow. Add flour; beat until smooth. Beat in evaporated milk and vanilla.

2. Pour batter into **CROCK-POT®** slow cooker. Place cherries evenly over batter. Cover; cook on LOW 3½ to 4 hours or until flan is set. Serve warm with whipped cream.

MAKES 6 SERVINGS

Spiced Vanilla Applesauce

Apple-Pecan Bread Pudding

8 cups bread, cubed

3 cups Granny Smith apples, cubed

1 cup chopped pecans

8 eggs

1 can (12 ounces) evaporated milk

1 cup packed brown sugar

½ cup apple cider or apple juice

2 teaspoons ground cinnamon

1 teaspoon ground nutmeg

1 teaspoon vanilla extract

½ teaspoon salt

½ teaspoon ground allspice

Ice cream

Caramel topping or whipped cream

1. Coat inside of **CROCK-POT**® slow cooker with nonstick cooking spray. Place bread cubes, apples and pecans in **CROCK-POT**® slow cooker.

2. Combine eggs, evaporated milk, brown sugar, apple cider, cinnamon, nutmeg, vanilla, salt and allspice in large bowl; stir to blend. Pour egg mixture into **CROCK-POT**® slow cooker. Cover; cook on LOW 3 hours. Serve with ice cream. Top with caramel sauce.

MAKES 8 SERVINGS

Brownie Bottoms

½ cup packed brown sugar

½ cup water

2 tablespoons unsweetened cocoa powder

2½ cups packaged brownie mix

1 package (2¾ ounces) instant chocolate pudding mix

½ cup milk chocolate chips

2 eggs, beaten

3 tablespoons butter or margarine, melted

Whipped cream or ice cream (optional)

1. Coat inside of **CROCK-POT**® slow cooker with nonstick cooking spray. Combine brown sugar, water and cocoa in small saucepan over medium heat; bring to a boil over medium-high heat.

2. Meanwhile, combine brownie mix, pudding mix, chocolate chips, eggs and butter in medium bowl; stir until well blended. Spread batter in **CROCK-POT**® slow cooker; pour boiling sugar mixture over batter.

3. Cover; cook on HIGH 1½ hours. Turn off heat. Let stand 30 minutes. Serve with whipped cream, if desired.

MAKES 6 SERVINGS

NOTE: Recipe can be doubled for a 5-, 6- or 7-quart **CROCK-POT**® slow cooker.

Five-Spice Apple Crisp

3 tablespoons unsalted butter, melted

6 Golden Delicious apples, peeled and cut into ½-inch-thick slices

2 teaspoons lemon juice

¼ cup packed brown sugar

¾ teaspoon Chinese five-spice powder, plus additional for garnish

1 cup coarsely crushed Chinese-style almond cookies or almond biscotti

Sweetened whipped cream (optional)

1. Butter inside of 4½-quart **CROCK-POT**® slow cooker with melted butter. Add apples and lemon juice; toss to combine. Sprinkle apples with brown sugar and ¾ teaspoon five-spice powder; toss again. Cover; cook on LOW 3½ hours.

2. Spoon into bowls. Sprinkle cookies over apples. Garnish with whipped cream and additional five-spice powder.

MAKES 4 SERVINGS

Chocolate Orange Fondue

½ cup whipping cream

1½ tablespoons butter

6 ounces 60 to 70% bittersweet chocolate, coarsely chopped

⅓ cup orange liqueur

¾ teaspoon vanilla

Marshmallows, strawberries and pound cake cubes

1. Bring whipping cream and butter to a boil in medium saucepan over medium heat. Remove from heat. Stir in chocolate, liqueur and vanilla until chocolate is melted. Place over medium-low heat; cook and stir 2 minutes until smooth.

2. Coat inside of **CROCK-POT® LITTLE DIPPER®** slow cooker with nonstick cooking spray. Fill with warm fondue. Serve with marshmallows, strawberries and pound cake cubes.

MAKES 1½ CUPS

Pumpkin-Cranberry Custard

1 can (30 ounces) pumpkin pie filling

1 can (12 ounces) evaporated milk

1 cup dried cranberries

4 eggs, beaten

1 cup whole gingersnap cookies (optional)

Combine pumpkin, evaporated milk, cranberries and eggs in **CROCK-POT®** slow cooker; stir to blend. Cover; cook on HIGH 4 to 4½ hours. Serve with gingersnaps, if desired.

MAKES 4 TO 6 SERVINGS

Chocolate Orange Fondue

Rustic Peach-Oat Crumble

8 cups frozen sliced peaches,
   thawed and juice reserved

¾ cup packed brown sugar, divided

1½ tablespoons cornstarch

1 tablespoon lemon juice (optional)

1½ teaspoons vanilla

½ teaspoon almond extract

1 cup quick oats

¼ cup all-purpose flour

¼ cup granulated sugar

1 teaspoon ground cinnamon

¼ teaspoon salt

½ cup (1 stick) cold butter, cut
   into pieces

1. Coat inside of 4½-quart **CROCK-POT**® slow cooker with nonstick cooking spray. Combine peaches with juice, ½ cup brown sugar, cornstarch, lemon juice, if desired, vanilla and almond extract in medium bowl; toss to coat. Place in **CROCK-POT**® slow cooker.

2. Combine oats, flour, remaining ¼ cup brown sugar, granulated sugar, cinnamon and salt in medium bowl. Cut in butter with pastry blender or two knives until mixture resembles coarse crumbs. Sprinkle over peaches. Cover; cook on HIGH 1½ hours or until bubbly at edge.

MAKES ABOUT 8 SERVINGS

S'mores Fondue

4 ounces semisweet chocolate chips

½ jar (about 3 ounces) marshmallow creme

3 tablespoons half-and-half

½ teaspoon vanilla

½ cup mini marshmallows

Bananas, strawberries, chocolate-covered pretzels, graham crackers and/or sliced apples

1. Combine chocolate chips, marshmallow creme and half-and-half in medium saucepan. Cook over medium heat 2 minutes or until melted and smooth, stirring constantly. Remove from heat. Stir in vanilla.

2. Coat inside of **CROCK-POT® LITTLE DIPPER®** slow cooker with nonstick cooking spray. Fill with warm fondue. Sprinkle with marshmallows. Serve with fruit, pretzels and graham crackers.

MAKES 1½ CUPS

Pumpkin Custard

1 cup solid-pack pumpkin
½ cup packed brown sugar
2 eggs, beaten
½ teaspoon ground ginger

½ teaspoon grated lemon peel
½ teaspoon ground cinnamon, plus additional for garnish
1 can (12 ounces) evaporated milk

1. Combine pumpkin, brown sugar, eggs, ginger, lemon peel and ½ teaspoon cinnamon in large bowl. Stir in evaporated milk. Divide mixture among six ramekins or custard cups. Cover each cup tightly with foil.

2. Place ramekins in **CROCK-POT**® slow cooker. Pour water into **CROCK-POT**® slow cooker to come about ½ inch from top of ramekins. Cover; cook on LOW 4 hours.

3. Use tongs or slotted spoon to remove ramekins from **CROCK-POT**® slow cooker. Sprinkle with additional ground cinnamon. Serve warm.

MAKES 6 SERVINGS

VARIATION: To make Pumpkin Custard in a single dish, pour custard into 1½-quart soufflé dish instead of ramekins. Cover with foil and place in **CROCK-POT**® slow cooker. (Place soufflé dish on two or three 18×2-inch strips of foil in **CROCK-POT**® slow cooker to make removal easier, if desired.) Add water to come 1½ inches from top of soufflé dish. Cover; cook as directed.

Poached Autumn Fruits with Vanilla-Citrus Broth

2 Granny Smith apples, peeled, cored and halved (reserve cores)

2 Bartlett pears, peeled, cored and halved (reserve cores)

1 orange, peeled and halved

⅓ cup sugar

5 tablespoons honey

1 vanilla bean, split and seeded (reserve seeds)

1 cinnamon stick

Vanilla ice cream (optional)

1. Place apple and pear cores in **CROCK-POT**® slow cooker. Squeeze juice from orange halves into **CROCK-POT**® slow cooker. Add orange halves, sugar, honey, vanilla bean and seeds and cinnamon stick. Add apples and pears. Pour in enough water to cover fruit; stir gently to combine. Cover; cook on HIGH 2 hours or until fruit is tender.

2. Remove apple and pear halves; set aside. Strain cooking liquid; discard solids. Cook, uncovered, on HIGH 10 to 15 minutes or until sauce is thickened.

3. Dice apple and pear halves. To serve, spoon fruit with sauce into bowls. Top with ice cream, if desired.

MAKES 4 TO 6 SERVINGS

Mexican Chocolate Bread Pudding

1½ cups whipping cream

4 ounces unsweetened chocolate, coarsely chopped

½ cup currants

2 eggs, beaten

½ cup sugar

1 teaspoon vanilla

¾ teaspoon ground cinnamon

½ teaspoon ground allspice

⅛ teaspoon salt

3 cups Hawaiian-style sweet bread, challah or rich egg bread, cut into ½-inch cubes

Whipped cream (optional)

Chopped macadamia nuts (optional)

1. Heat whipping cream in large saucepan. Add chocolate; stir until melted.

2. Combine currants, eggs, sugar, vanilla, cinnamon, allspice and salt in medium bowl; stir to blend. Add currant mixture to chocolate mixture; stir well to combine. Pour into **CROCK-POT**® slow cooker.

3. Gently fold in bread cubes using plastic spatula. Cover; cook on HIGH 3 to 4 hours or until knife inserted near center comes out clean. Top with whipped cream and sprinkle with nuts, if desired.

MAKES 6 TO 8 SERVINGS

Classic Baked Apples

¼ cup packed dark brown sugar

2 tablespoons golden raisins

1 teaspoon grated lemon peel

6 small to medium baking apples, cored

1 teaspoon ground cinnamon, plus additional for garnish

2 tablespoons butter, cubed

¼ cup orange juice

¼ cup water

Whipped cream (optional)

1. Combine brown sugar, raisins and lemon peel in small bowl; stir to blend. Fill core of each apple with mixture. Place apples in **CROCK-POT**® slow cooker. Sprinkle with 1 teaspoon cinnamon; dot with butter. Pour orange juice and water over apples.

2. Cover; cook on LOW 7 to 9 hours or on HIGH 2½ to 3½ hours. Place apples in individual bowls; top with sauce. Garnish with whipped cream; sprinkled with additional cinnamon.

MAKES 6 SERVINGS

Cherry Delight

1 can (21 ounces) cherry pie filling

1 package (about 18 ounces) yellow cake mix

½ cup (1 stick) butter, melted

⅓ cup chopped walnuts

Place pie filling in **CROCK-POT**® slow cooker. Combine cake mix and butter in medium bowl. Spread evenly over pie filling. Sprinkle with walnuts. Cover; cook on LOW 3 to 4 hours or on HIGH 1½ to 2 hours.

MAKES 8 TO 10 SERVINGS

Classic Baked Apples

Citrus Chinese Dates
with Toasted Hazelnuts

2 cups pitted dates

⅔ cup boiling water

½ cup sugar

Peel from 1 lemon (yellow part only)

¼ cup hazelnuts, shelled and toasted*

Whipped cream (optional)

To toast hazelnuts, spread in single layer in heavy skillet. Cook over medium heat 1 to 2 minutes or until nuts are lightly browned, stirring frequently.

1. Place dates in medium bowl; cover with water. Soak overnight to rehydrate. Drain, and remove dates to **CROCK-POT**® slow cooker.

2. Add ⅔ cup boiling water, sugar and lemon peel to **CROCK-POT**® slow cooker. Cover; cook on HIGH 3 hours.

3. Remove and discard peel. Place dates in serving dishes. Sprinkle with hazelnuts. Top with whipped cream, if desired.

MAKES 4 SERVINGS

Delicious Desserts

Cinnamon-Ginger Poached Pears

3 cups water

1 cup sugar

10 slices fresh ginger

2 whole cinnamon sticks

1 tablespoon chopped candied ginger (optional)

6 Bosc or Anjou pears, peeled and cored

1. Combine water, sugar, fresh ginger, cinnamon and candied ginger, if desired, in **CROCK-POT**® slow cooker. Add pears. Cover; cook on LOW 4 to 6 hours or on HIGH 1½ to 2 hours.

2. Remove pears with slotted spoon. Cook syrup, uncovered, on HIGH 30 minutes or until thickened. Remove and discard cinnamon sticks.

MAKES 6 SERVINGS

Dulce de Leche

1 can (14 ounces) sweetened condensed milk

Bananas, apples, shortbread, chocolate wafers, pretzels and/or waffle cookies

Pour sweetened condensed milk into 9×5-inch loaf pan. Cover tightly with foil. Place loaf pan in **CROCK-POT**® slow cooker. Pour enough water to reach halfway up sides of loaf pan. Cover; cook on LOW 5 to 6 hours or until golden and thickened. Serve with bananas, apples, shortbread, chocolate wafers, pretzels and/or waffle cookies.

MAKES ABOUT 1½ CUPS

Cinnamon-Ginger Poached Pears

Plum Bread Pudding

1 loaf (1 pound) sliced egg bread, lightly toasted*

2 tablespoons unsalted butter, divided

12 large unpeeled Italian plums, pitted and cut into wedges (about 4 cups total), divided

1½ cups plus 2 tablespoons sugar, divided

3 cups half-and-half

10 eggs

1¼ cups milk

2 teaspoons vanilla

¾ teaspoon salt

¾ teaspoon ground cinnamon

Sweetened whipped cream or vanilla ice cream (optional)

*Use an egg-rich bread, such as challah, for best results. For a more delicate bread pudding, substitute cinnamon rolls or plain Danish rolls.

1. Coat inside of 6-quart **CROCK-POT**® slow cooker with nonstick cooking spray. Cut toasted bread into 1-inch cubes; set aside.

2. Melt 1 tablespoon butter in large skillet over medium-high heat. Add half of sliced plums and 1 tablespoon sugar; cook 2 minutes or until plums are pulpy and release their juices. Pour plums and juices into medium bowl; repeat with remaining 1 tablespoon butter, remaining plums and 1 tablespoon sugar. Set aside.

3. Beat half-and-half, eggs, remaining 1½ cups sugar, milk, vanilla, salt and cinnamon in large bowl. Stir in bread, plums and any accumulated juices. Spoon into **CROCK-POT**® slow cooker. Cover; cook on HIGH 3 hours or until pudding is firm when gently shaken and thin knife inserted halfway between center and edge comes out clean. Turn off heat. Let cool 15 minutes. Serve with whipped cream, if desired.

MAKES 12 TO 16 SERVINGS

PEACH BREAD PUDDING: If fresh plums are not available, substitute 9 large peaches, peeled, pitted and cut into wedges or 4 cups frozen sliced peaches, thawed (juices reserved).

Delicious Desserts

Cinnamon Roll-Topped Mixed Berry Cobbler

2 bags (12 ounces *each*) frozen mixed berries, thawed

1 cup sugar

¼ cup quick-cooking tapioca

¼ cup water

2 teaspoons vanilla

1 package (about 12 ounces) refrigerated cinnamon rolls with icing

Combine berries, sugar, tapioca, water and vanilla in **CROCK-POT**® slow cooker; top with cinnamon rolls. Cover; cook on LOW 4 to 5 hours. Serve warm, drizzled with icing.

MAKES 8 SERVINGS

NOTE: This recipe was designed to work best in a 4-quart **CROCK-POT**® slow cooker. Double the ingredients for larger **CROCK-POT**® slow cookers, but always place cinnamon rolls in a single layer.

Warm Spiced Apples and Pears

½ cup (1 stick) butter
1 vanilla bean
1 cup packed brown sugar
½ cup water
½ lemon, sliced

1 cinnamon stick, broken in half
½ teaspoon ground cloves
5 pears, quartered and cored
5 small Granny Smith apples, cored and quartered

1. Melt butter in medium saucepan over medium heat. Cut vanilla bean in half and scrape out seeds. Add seeds and pod, brown sugar, water, lemon slices, cinnamon stick and cloves to saucepan. Bring to a boil; cook 1 minute, stirring constantly. Remove from heat.

2. Combine pears, apples and butter mixture in **CROCK-POT**® slow cooker; stir to blend. Cover; cook on LOW 3½ to 4 hours or on HIGH 2 hours. Stir every 45 minutes. Remove and discard vanilla pod and cinnamon stick before serving.

MAKES 6 SERVINGS

Strawberry Rhubarb Crisp

4 cups sliced hulled strawberries

4 cups diced rhubarb (about 5 stalks), cut into ½-inch dice

2 cups granulated sugar, divided

2 tablespoons lemon juice

1½ tablespoons cornstarch, plus water (optional)

1 cup all-purpose flour

1 cup old-fashioned oats

½ cup packed brown sugar

½ teaspoon ground ginger

½ teaspoon ground nutmeg

½ cup (1 stick) butter, cut into pieces

½ cup sliced almonds, toasted*

To toast almonds, spread in single layer in heavy skillet. Cook over medium heat 1 to 2 minutes or until nuts are lightly browned, stirring frequently.

1. Coat inside of **CROCK-POT**® slow cooker with nonstick cooking spray. Combine strawberries, rhubarb, 1½ cups granulated sugar and lemon juice in **CROCK-POT**® slow cooker; stir to blend. Cover; cook on HIGH 1½ hours or until fruit is tender.

2. If fruit is dry after cooking, add a little water. If fruit has too much liquid, mix cornstarch with a little water and stir into liquid. Cook, uncovered, on HIGH 15 minutes or until cooking liquid is thickened.

3. Combine flour, oats, remaining ½ cup granulated sugar, brown sugar, ginger and nutmeg in medium bowl. Cut in butter using pastry blender or two knives until mixture resembles coarse crumbs. Stir in almonds.

4. Remove lid from **CROCK-POT**® slow cooker and gently sprinkle topping onto fruit. Cook, uncovered, on HIGH 10 to 15 minutes or until topping is heated through.

MAKES 8 SERVINGS

Bananas Foster

12 bananas, cut into quarters
1 cup flaked coconut
1 cup dark corn syrup
⅔ cup butter, melted
¼ cup lemon juice
2 teaspoons grated lemon peel

2 teaspoons rum
1 teaspoon ground cinnamon
½ teaspoon salt
12 slices pound cake
1 quart vanilla ice cream

1. Combine bananas and coconut in **CROCK-POT**® slow cooker. Stir corn syrup, butter, lemon juice, lemon peel, rum, cinnamon and salt in medium bowl; pour over bananas.

2. Cover; cook on LOW 1 to 2 hours. To serve, arrange bananas on pound cake slices. Top with ice cream and warm sauce.

MAKES 12 SERVINGS

Pumpkin Bread Pudding

2 cups whole milk

½ cup (1 stick) plus 2 tablespoons butter, divided

1 cup packed brown sugar, divided

1 cup solid-pack pumpkin

3 eggs

1 tablespoon ground cinnamon

2 teaspoons vanilla

½ teaspoon ground nutmeg

¼ teaspoon salt

16 slices cinnamon raisin bread, torn into small pieces (8 cups total)

½ cup whipping cream

2 tablespoons bourbon (optional)

1. Coat inside of **CROCK-POT**® slow cooker with nonstick cooking spray. Combine milk and 2 tablespoons butter in medium microwavable bowl. Microwave on HIGH 2½ to 3 minutes.

2. Whisk ½ cup brown sugar, pumpkin, eggs, cinnamon, vanilla, nutmeg and salt in large bowl until well blended. Whisk in milk mixture until blended. Add bread cubes; toss to coat. Remove bread mixture to **CROCK-POT**® slow cooker.

3. Cover; cook on HIGH 2 hours or until knife inserted in center comes out clean. Turn off heat. Uncover; let stand 15 minutes.

4. Combine remaining ½ cup butter, remaining ½ cup brown sugar and whipping cream in small saucepan; bring to a boil over high heat, stirring frequently. Remove from heat. Stir in bourbon, if desired. Spoon bread pudding into individual bowls; top with sauce.

MAKES 8 SERVINGS

Tequila-Poached Pears

4 Anjou pears, peeled

2 cups water

1 can (11½ ounces) pear nectar

1 cup tequila

½ cup sugar

Grated peel and juice of 1 lime

Vanilla ice cream (optional)

1. Place pears in **CROCK-POT**® slow cooker. Combine water, nectar, tequila, sugar, lime peel and lime juice in medium saucepan. Bring to a boil over medium-high heat, stirring frequently. Boil 1 minute; pour over pears.

2. Cover; cook on LOW 4 to 6 hours or on HIGH 2 to 3 hours or until pears are tender. Serve warm with poaching liquid and ice cream, if desired.

MAKES 4 SERVINGS

TIP: Poaching fruit in a sugar, juice or alcohol syrup helps the fruit retain its shape and become more flavorful.

Figs Poached in Red Wine

2 cups dry red wine

1 cup packed brown sugar

12 dried Calimyrna or Mediterranean figs (about 6 ounces)

2 (3-inch) whole cinnamon sticks

1 teaspoon finely grated orange peel

4 tablespoons whipping cream (optional)

1. Combine wine, brown sugar, figs, cinnamon sticks and orange peel in **CROCK-POT**® slow cooker; stir to blend. Cover; cook on LOW 5 to 6 hours or on HIGH 4 to 5 hours.

2. Remove and discard cinnamon sticks. To serve, spoon figs and syrup onto serving dish. Top with whipping cream, if desired.

MAKES 4 SERVINGS

Peaches and Cream Melange

2 tablespoons unsalted butter

¾ cup buttermilk baking mix

⅓ cup granulated sugar

¼ cup packed brown sugar

2 eggs

2 teaspoons vanilla

2 cups fresh ripe peaches, pitted, peeled and mashed

1 cup light cream

1 tablespoon butter, melted

1 teaspoon ground cinnamon

1 teaspoon ground nutmeg

Butter inside of **CROCK-POT**® slow cooker with 2 tablespoons unsalted butter. Combine baking mix, granulated sugar and brown sugar in large bowl. Add eggs and vanilla; stir well to combine. Add peaches, cream, 1 tablespoon melted butter, cinnamon and nutmeg; stir well to combine. Pour into **CROCK-POT**® slow cooker. Cover; cook on LOW 6 to 8 hours or on HIGH 3 to 4 hours.

MAKES 4 SERVINGS

Figs Poached in Red Wine

Bittersweet Chocolate-Espresso Crème Brûlée

½ cup chopped bittersweet chocolate

5 egg yolks

1½ cups whipping cream

½ cup granulated sugar

¼ cup espresso

¼ cup Demerara or raw sugar

1. Arrange five 6-ounce ramekins or custard cups inside **CROCK-POT**® slow cooker. Pour enough water to come halfway up sides of ramekins (taking care to keep water out of ramekins). Divide chocolate among ramekins.

2. Whisk egg yolks in small bowl; set aside. Heat small saucepan over medium heat. Add cream, granulated sugar and espresso; cook and stir until mixture begins to boil. Pour hot cream mixture in thin, steady stream into egg yolks, whisking constantly. Pour through fine mesh strainer into clean bowl.

3. Ladle into prepared ramekins in bottom of **CROCK-POT**® slow cooker. Cover; cook on HIGH 1 to 2 hours or until custard is set around edges but still soft in centers.

4. Carefully remove ramekins; cool to room temperature. Cover; refrigerate until serving. Spread tops of custards with Demerara sugar just before serving.

MAKES 5 SERVINGS

Pineapple Rice Pudding

1 can (20 ounces) crushed
   pineapple in juice, undrained

1 can (about 13 ounces)
   unsweetened coconut milk

1 can (12 ounces) evaporated milk

¾ cup uncooked Arborio rice

2 eggs, lightly beaten

¼ cup granulated sugar

¼ cup packed brown sugar

½ teaspoon ground cinnamon

¼ teaspoon salt

¼ teaspoon ground nutmeg

   Toasted coconut and pineapple
   slices (optional)*

*To toast coconut, spread in single layer
in small heavy-bottomed skillet. Cook and
stir over medium heat 1 to 2 minutes or
until lightly browned. Remove from skillet
immediately.*

1. Combine crushed pineapple with juice, coconut milk, evaporated milk, rice, eggs, granulated sugar, brown sugar, cinnamon, salt and nutmeg in **CROCK-POT**® slow cooker; stir to blend. Cover; cook on HIGH 3 to 4 hours or until thickened and rice is tender.

2. Stir to blend. Serve warm or chilled. Garnish with toasted coconut and pineapple slices.

MAKES 8 SERVINGS

Index

METRIC CONVERSION CHART

VOLUME MEASUREMENTS (dry)

$^1/_8$ teaspoon = 0.5 mL
$^1/_4$ teaspoon = 1 mL
$^1/_2$ teaspoon = 2 mL
$^3/_4$ teaspoon = 4 mL
1 teaspoon = 5 mL
1 tablespoon = 15 mL
2 tablespoons = 30 mL
$^1/_4$ cup = 60 mL
$^1/_3$ cup = 75 mL
$^1/_2$ cup = 125 mL
$^2/_3$ cup = 150 mL
$^3/_4$ cup = 175 mL
1 cup = 250 mL
2 cups = 1 pint = 500 mL
3 cups = 750 mL
4 cups = 1 quart = 1 L

VOLUME MEASUREMENTS (fluid)

1 fluid ounce (2 tablespoons) = 30 mL
4 fluid ounces ($^1/_2$ cup) = 125 mL
8 fluid ounces (1 cup) = 250 mL
12 fluid ounces (1$^1/_2$ cups) = 375 mL
16 fluid ounces (2 cups) = 500 mL

WEIGHTS (mass)

$^1/_2$ ounce = 15 g
1 ounce = 30 g
3 ounces = 90 g
4 ounces = 120 g
8 ounces = 225 g
10 ounces = 285 g
12 ounces = 360 g
16 ounces = 1 pound = 450 g

DIMENSIONS

$^1/_{16}$ inch = 2 mm
$^1/_8$ inch = 3 mm
$^1/_4$ inch = 6 mm
$^1/_2$ inch = 1.5 cm
$^3/_4$ inch = 2 cm
1 inch = 2.5 cm

OVEN TEMPERATURES

250°F = 120°C
275°F = 140°C
300°F = 150°C
325°F = 160°C
350°F = 180°C
375°F = 190°C
400°F = 200°C
425°F = 220°C
450°F = 230°C

BAKING PAN SIZES

Utensil	Size in Inches/Quarts	Metric Volume	Size in Centimeters
Baking or	$8\times8\times2$	2 L	$20\times20\times5$
Cake Pan	$9\times9\times2$	2.5 L	$23\times23\times5$
(square or	$12\times8\times2$	3 L	$30\times20\times5$
rectangular)	$13\times9\times2$	3.5 L	$33\times23\times5$
Loaf Pan	$8\times4\times3$	1.5 L	$20\times10\times7$
	$9\times5\times3$	2 L	$23\times13\times7$
Round Layer	$8\times1^1/_2$	1.2 L	20×4
Cake Pan	$9\times1^1/_2$	1.5 L	23×4
Pie Plate	$8\times1^1/_4$	750 mL	20×3
	$9\times1^1/_4$	1 L	23×3
Baking Dish	1 quart	1 L	—
or Casserole	1$^1/_2$ quart	1.5 L	—
	2 quart	2 L	—